W9-AYF-103

Walks in the *Country* Near *LONDON*

The Joint Free Public Library
of
Morristown and Morris Township

Walks in the *Country* Near *LONDON*

CHRISTOPHER SOMERVILLE

Interlink Books

An imprint of Interlink Publishing Group, Inc.
Northampton

First American edition published 2004 by

INTERLINK BOOKS
An imprint of Interlink Publishing Group, Inc.
46 Crosby Street, Northampton, Massachusetts 01060
www.interlinkbooks.com

Text copyright © 2004 Christopher Somerville
Photography copyright © 2004 by individual photographers credited on page 208

All rights reserved. No part of this publication may be reproduced, stored in a
retrieval system or transmitted, in any form or by any means, electronic, mechanical,
photocopying, recording or otherwise, without the prior written permission of the publishers.

ISBN 1-56656-528-6

Reproduction by Pica Digital (Pte) Ltd, Singapore
Printed and bound in Singapore by Kyodo Printing Co (Singapore) Pte Ltd

Front cover: Walkers enjoy a stroll in the sunshine along the Thames Path National Trail near Goring on
the Oxfordshire/Berkshire border.

This book is dedicated with warm affection to Howard Richmond and Robin Rubenstein and their
sons Matthew and Michael, hoping that they will venture out of London to
enjoy these walks.

Publishers' Note: While every care has been taken to ensure that the information in this book was as
accurate as possible at the time of going to press, the publishers and author accept no responsibility for
any loss, injury or inconvenience sustained by anyone using this book.

To request our complete 40-page full-color catalog,
please call us toll free at **1-800-238-LINK,** visit our website at **www.interlinkbooks.com**, or write to
Interlink Publishing
46 Crosby Street, Northampton, MA 01060
e-mail: sales@interlinkbooks.com

CONTENTS

KEY TO MAPS

Each of the walks in the book is accompanied by a map on which the route is shown in blue. Places of interest along the walk, such as historic buildings, churches and pubs, are clearly identified. Where necessary, specific route directions have also been included on the maps. In both the text and the maps certain features and national trails have been abbreviated as follows:

FP	Footpath	SHT	Swale Heritage Trail
PB	Public Bridleway	NDW	North Downs Way
BW	Byway	GW	Greensand Way
PH	Public House	GWLR	Greensand Way Link Route
NT	National Trust	SVW	Stour Valley Walk
BT	John Bunyan Trail	MVW	Medway Valley Walk
IW	Icknield Way	EVW	Eden Valley Walk
CW	Chiltern Way	VW	Vanguard Way
EW	Essex Way	PW	Pilgrims' Way
RVW	Roach Valley Way	HW	Hangers Way
DVP	Darent Valley Path	WW	Wayfarer's Walk

Although every effort has been taken to ensure that these maps are clear and correct, Ordnance Survey grid references are provided at key parts of the route for each walk. Details of relevant Ordnance Survey maps are supplied at the start of each walk.

The following is a key to the symbols used on the maps.

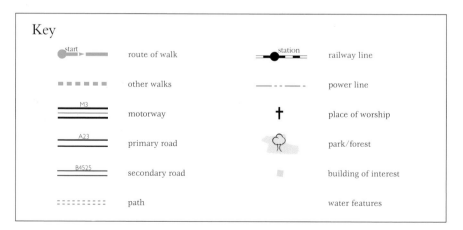

Key

route of walk	railway line
other walks	power line
motorway (M3)	place of worship
primary road (A23)	park/forest
secondary road (B4525)	building of interest
path	water features

INTRODUCTION

Just about had it up to *here* with London? Fed up to the back teeth with jostling streets, polluted air, the prison-like grey of hard stone and concrete, the constant rush and hassle? Do you dream of escaping to the countryside with its uncrowded green lanes and field paths, of following sun-dappled ways through woods full of bird song, of high open downland where you can stroll all day under enormous skies and breathe clean air? How about a bite to eat in a village pub? Not a snatched sandwich, gobbled under pressure at a work desk or computer screen, but a leisurely lunch which you have earned over a morning's ramble through gorgeous country. Do you like the idea of having so much time to spare that you can stop for an hour or so to explore a fascinating Norman church or a moated castle with its ghosts, romance and wild history?

All this is waiting for you, in less time than it takes to get from Leicester Square to Piccadilly Circus in the rush hour. Just hop on a train at any one of a dozen central London stations with this book in your hand, and within an hour or so you can be setting out on a beautiful, invigorating country walk. There are 25 rural rambles in *Walks in the Country Near London* – each one based on a railway station, so that you don't even have to think about driving. The most that you will see or hear of the capital is the occasional far-off glimpse on one or two of the walks. Other than that, you'll be walking deep in the Chiltern countryside of Oxfordshire, Buckinghamshire, Bedfordshire and Hertfordshire, the rolling farmlands and lonely marsh rivers of back-country Essex, the chalk and greensand downs of the Kent and Sussex Weald, and the woods, downs and heaths of Surrey, Hampshire and Berkshire.

These country rambles are not designed for masochistic tread-till-you're-dead hikers. Almost all the walks are between 6 and 10 miles (10–16km) – a morning's worth if you are reasonably fit and don't want to stop en route, an easy day if you are going to take your time and explore a bit. A couple of longer walks have been included for those who are in need of a good stride out. Be warned, however, that outside of the summer months and in wet conditions, several of the walks can be very muddy and waterproof footwear is highly recommended.

You don't need to be a navigation expert: the comprehensive instructions have been carefully designed, not just to steer experienced country walkers from one village to the next, but to get complete beginners from one stile to the next. The Ordnance Survey of Great Britain produces far and away the best walkers' maps in the world, and you are strongly advised to take the relevant OS map to supplement the sketch maps provided in this book.

Advice on exactly which OS map you'll need is included in the information section at the head of each walk. The Explorer series covers the area at twice the scale of the Landranger series, and also includes field boundaries and much other helpful detail. Ordnance Survey national grid reference numbers are included within the text at all points where you might need to check your position on the map. If you want to slip a compass into your pocket, it might be reassuring – though not really necessary.

Distances should be treated as approximate – for example: 'In 100 yards (100m) turn left' does not mean a distance exactly measured at 100 yards rather than 99 or 101, but 100 rather than 50 or 150. By the same token, conversion from imperial to metric measurements and vice versa is also approximate. One hundred yards is actually 91 metres, but I hope you know what I mean by '100 yards (100m)'!

Other useful advice given in each information section includes the length of the walk, where you start and finish, how to get there from central London by rail (and by road, if you must), where you can get a drink and something to eat en route, and the various special features and attractions along the way. More detailed information, including addresses, telephone numbers, websites and opening hours, is given in Further Information (pages 192–201) for features open to the public, such as stately homes, castles, museums and pubs. It's a wise plan to phone before you set out to double-check on prices, opening and food-serving times, as these can and do change. Don't forget to carry your National Trust, English Heritage and other membership cards that give you free entry, as several of the attractions are run by these organisations. Many of the most beautiful and interesting churches are kept locked; contact details are given for these, too, so that with a little forward planning you can get in.

I have personally walked every yard of these 25 rambles. However, since things in the countryside change all the time, it is possible that small details may have altered by the time you set out. If so, or if you find any other inaccuracies in this book, please let me know via the publishers. I will gladly acknowledge your help and incorporate your amendments in any future editions of *Walks in the Country Near London.*

Have a wonderful time!

Christopher Somerville

Opposite: Footpath fingerposts, like this one on the Ridgeway National Trail, point the way for experienced hikers and complete beginners alike.

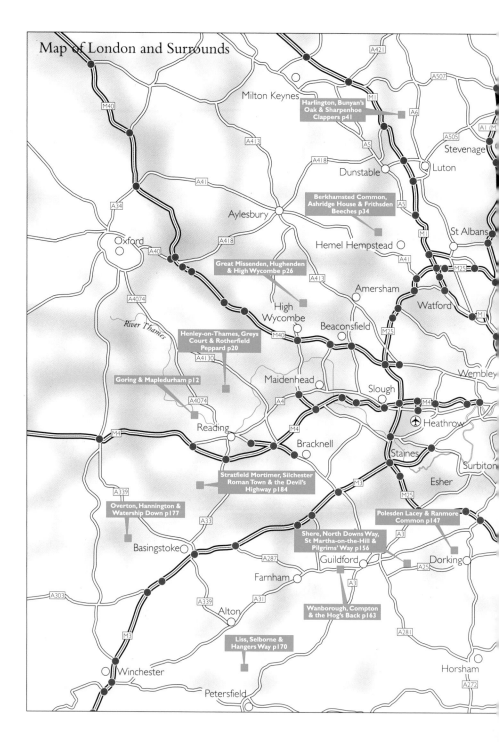

Map of London and Surrounds

Milton Keynes

Harlington, Bunyan's Oak & Sharpenhoe Clappers p41

Stevenage

Dunstable

Luton

St Albans

Berkhamsted Common, Ashridge House & Frithsden Beeches p34

Aylesbury

Hemel Hempstead

Oxford

Great Missenden, Hughenden & High Wycombe p26

Amersham

Watford

High Wycombe

Beaconsfield

Wembley

River Thames

Henley-on-Thames, Greys Court & Rotherfield Peppard p20

Maidenhead

Slough

Goring & Mapledurham p12

Reading

Heathrow

Bracknell

Staines

Surbiton

Stratfield Mortimer, Silchester Roman Town & the Devil's Highway p184

Esher

Overton, Hannington & Watership Down p177

Polesden Lacey & Ranmore Common p147

Shere, North Downs Way, St Martha-on-the-Hill & Pilgrims' Way p156

Basingstoke

Guildford

Dorking

Farnham

Alton

Wanborough, Compton & the Hog's Back p163

Liss, Selborne & Hangers Way p170

Winchester

Horsham

Petersfield

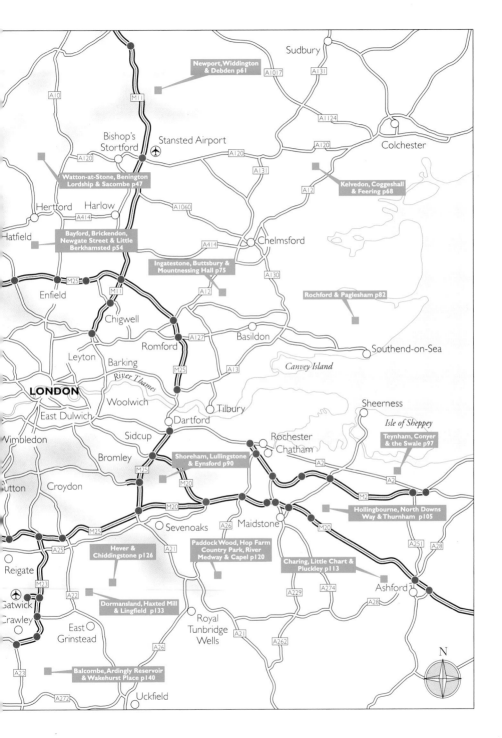

Newport, Widdington & Debden p61

Sudbury

Colchester

A1017

A131

A1124

A10

M11

A120

A120

Bishop's Stortford

Stansted Airport

A120

A131

A2

A131

Watton-at-Stone, Benington Lordship & Sacombe p47

Kelvedon, Coggeshall & Feering p68

Hertford

Harlow

A1060

A414

Hatfield

Bayford, Brickendon, Newgate Street & Little Berkhamsted p54

A414

Chelmsford

Ingatestone, Buttsbury & Mountnessing Hall p75

A130

M25

M11

A12

Rochford & Paglesham p82

Enfield

Chigwell

Romford

A127

Basildon

Southend-on-Sea

Leyton

Barking

A13

Canvey Island

M25

River Thames

LONDON

Woolwich

Tilbury

Sheerness

East Dulwich

Dartford

Isle of Sheppey

Wimbledon

Sidcup

Rochester

Chatham

Teynham, Conyer & the Swale p97

Bromley

Shoreham, Lullingstone & Eynsford p90

A2

M25

M20

A2

M2

Sutton

Croydon

M20

Hollingbourne, North Downs Way & Thurnham p105

M25

Sevenoaks

A26

Maidstone

M20

A251

A28

Hever & Chiddingstone p126

A21

Paddock Wood, Hop Farm Country Park, River Medway & Capel p120

Charing, Little Chart & Pluckley p113

Reigate

M23

A22

A229

A274

Ashford

A28

Gatwick

Crawley

Dormansland, Haxted Mill & Lingfield p133

A25

Royal Tunbridge Wells

A21

A262

East Grinstead

A26

N

A23

Balcombe, Ardingly Reservoir & Wakehurst Place p140

Uckfield

A272

11

GORING & MAPLEDURHAM

Enjoy the beech and oak woods, the lush green grazing meadows and the glorious river scenery along a most delectable stretch of the Thames Valley. Take a break in the beautifully preserved old village of Mapledurham, and visit the lovely and atmospheric Elizabethan country house where Roman Catholic priests were hidden in times of persecution. Kenneth Grahame used Mapledurham House as inspiration for Toad Hall in *The Wind in the Willows*, and the book's illustrator Ernest Shepard based several of his pictures on the old mill and weir. This twist of countryside, where the Thames snakes through the narrow confines of the Goring Gap and on towards Reading, was one of Grahame's favourite parts of the river; he lies buried in Pangbourne.

Start:	Goring and Streatley Station
Finish:	Pangbourne Station
Length of walk:	12 miles (20km)
OS maps:	1:50,000 Landranger 175; 1:25,000 Explorer 170, 159
Travel:	By rail from London Paddington (49 mins); by road – M25 (Jct 15), M4 (Jct 12), A1 through Theale for 1 mile (1.6km), A340 to Pangbourne, A329 to Goring.
Features:	Thames Path National Trail; Goring Gap; views along the Thames; Isambard Kingdom Brunel's railway bridge at Gatehampton; Bottom Wood and Bottom Farm; Mapledurham House and Mill and village; Whitchurch Toll Bridge; Pangbourne.
Refreshments:	King Charles Head PH, Collinsend Common; Mapledurham House tea-room; pubs and cafés in Goring, Whitchurch and Pangbourne.

Opposite: The watermill at Mapledurham, which dates back to medieval times, is said to have inspired Ernest Shepard's illustrations to Kenneth Grahame's famous children's book The Wind in the Willows.

THE WALK

From Goring and Streatley railway station (603806) walk up the approach road and keep ahead, to bear left in 200 yards (200m) across the railway bridge and down to the bridge over the River Thames (596808). This river crossing between Goring and Streatley is an ancient one. The prehistoric Ridgeway or Icknield Way fords the Thames here, and a ferry of sorts was

operating from the time of King Henry I in the early 12th century. There are some fine old Georgian houses across the river in Streatley.

Thames Path National Trail

Opposite the Riverside Tea Room a slip road leads to the left, down beside the bridge and onto the Thames Path National Trail. From this point for the next 3½ miles (5.5km) to Whitchurch, navigation is easy – just follow the Thames Path waymarks. The Thames Path in its entirety shadows the course of the river for 180 miles from its humble source in a Gloucestershire meadow to the beginning of its great estuary at the Thames Flood Barrier in east London. The National Trail was officially opened in 1996, after almost a century's attempts to establish some kind of acknowledged route for walkers along the old towpath. The path frequently jumps from bank to bank (as it does here at Goring), mirroring the efforts of the Thames Commissioners in past centuries to forge a continuous towpath while avoiding the property of antagonistic riparians.

The Goring Gap

The path runs south from Goring along the east bank of the Thames, passing large Edwardian houses with beautifully kept lawns. You enter open countryside of broad grazing meadows, and soon pass under an impressive Victorian railway bridge in warm red brick blotched with lichens and stained by the weather (606796). It carries Isambard Kingdom Brunel's Great Western Railway line across the Thames, to squeeze with the river through the Goring Gap. This cleft in the chalk hills was forced through by rushing meltwater after the end of the last Ice Age. Once the breakthrough had occurred, the meltwaters cut a narrow gorge in the chalk which gradually broadened out, perhaps 6,000 years ago. The Gap has the effect of pulling the downs dramatically close all of a sudden – the Berkshire Downs to the right across the river, and the Oxfordshire outliers of the Chiltern Hills at your left hand.

The path skirts the old ferry cottage at Gatehampton and continues in chalk woodland for a really beautiful mile (1.6km), with glimpses through the trees to the river below, before swinging inland (621786) through the southern shank of Hartslock Wood. Once out of the trees the Thames Path runs for a mile (1.6km) across the downs, at first as a track and then as a rough farm drive, before reaching the B471 (633775) ½ mile (0.75km) north of Whitchurch Toll Bridge. Turn left here up the road (please be aware of road traffic and take care!) for some 400 yards (400m), and at a right-hand bend (633780) keep ahead through woodland on a footpath. In 400 yards (400m) you emerge and aim ahead to pass Beech Farm (634787). Cross the drive and the paddock beyond, turning right at a kissing gate to follow the outside edge of a wood to the farm drive. Keep ahead to turn right along the B471 (637789).

In 150 yards (150m), opposite a thatched cottage, bear left; in 50 yards (50m), turn left again at a T-junction; in another 50 yards (50m), head right (FP sign on left side of the road) down a gravelly track. Pass a terrace of cottages, go through a kissing gate and follow the path across a field to the far left corner, where you bear right along a track (641786). There follows an exceptionally mucky short stretch as the track passes a pig farm; but the pigs, as pigs tend to do, look cheerful enough. In 250 yards (250m) the muck ends; keep ahead through a gate with two yellow arrow waymarks, following the one pointing ahead and keeping a fence on your right. The next field ends at a lane (647785); bear right here to meet a road (649784). Turn left. In 300 yards (300m), at a sharp left bend (652785), bear right ('Path, Hill Farm' sign). In 100 yards (100m), where the road swings right, keep ahead ('Collins End ½' FP sign) through trees, dropping steeply down into a valley only to climb steeply up the other side, aiming for a house on the skyline.

Collinsend Common and the King Charles Head PH

At the top of the rise, 50 yards (50m) before the house, turn right across a stile, then left through a gate to a lane (657787) where you turn right. At Holmes's Farm, a 'Bridleway, Mapledurham 2' sign directs you forward, with a fence on your right, to a gate into a tarmac lane by Holly Copse house (661785) on the edge of Goring Heath. The whole area of Goring Heath was enclosed in 1812, depriving the commoners of their right to graze animals on common land. The thin scatter of houses across Collinsend Common, just beyond Holly Copse, shows how building went on all over the open land.

If you would like pub refreshment, turn left along the lane past Briar Cottage for 150 yards (150m); then turn right between fences and across stiles (yellow arrows) for ¼ mile (0.4km) to the road and the King Charles Head (664789), a very friendly public house with plenty of attractive beams and good food and beer.

Back at Holly Copse, follow the track past the house, bearing right (blue PB arrow) between Holly Copse house on the right and Holly Copse Cottage on the left, onto a gravel bridleway (soon turning chalky) that descends through the woods. At a meeting of tracks in the wood bottom (663783) bear left (forked white arrow on tree) on a bridleway, at first very boggy but soon improving. Leave the wood at a gate (666781), keeping ahead south-east along a valley. In ½ mile (0.75km) pass Bottom Farm (672776) and continue south along the drive to a road (672773); keep ahead here to pass The White House (671770) and walk through Mapledurham village to Mapledurham House (670766).

Mapledurham House and Mill

A timber-framed 14th-century manor house stands on the site, but it is overshadowed by the great Tudor house built of red brick in 1580 by

Michael Blount, courtier and Lieutenant of the Tower. Blount was a devout Roman Catholic, and must have been held in enormously high favour by Queen Elizabeth I to have been allowed to build himself such a sumptuous house at a time in English history when men of his religion were held to be no better than traitors. He was no trimmer, though. Many a brave priest infiltrating England from the Continent, at risk of a horrible death upon capture, came warily upriver to Mapledurham. One of the house's high gables overlooking the Thames is still studded with the oyster shells that were fixed there as a sign of a recusant or staunchly Catholic house. Mapledurham House stands only 50 yards (50m) from the river, and could offer safe hiding for fugitives among its secret rooms and craftily hidden compartments. These included a noxious hole next to the privy – hard to bear for a man cooped up there for days on end, but guaranteed to put off sniffer dogs.

On a tour of the house, along with elaborate 17th-century plasterwork and portraits of the dark-faced Blounts, you can see some of the many hidey holes and a secret chapel under the eaves which would, if discovered, have got Michael Blount into very serious – probably terminal – trouble. There is also a much more luxurious chapel built in the 1790s in fashionable Strawberry Hill Gothic style. Horrific accounts of the bloodbaths accompanying the French Revolution had helped make the English more sympathetic to Catholic refugees, and no-one raised objections when the Blounts invested in a new chapel to accommodate the many French emigrés who were making their way to Mapledurham in expectation of help and support.

The medieval water-mill opposite the house was picturesque enough to inspire Ernest Shepard when he was looking for ideas for his marvellous illustrations to Kenneth Grahame's 1908 children's classic *The Wind in the Willows*. Some say that Grahame based Toad Hall upon Mapledurham. These days the restored mill grinds flour with the help of its oaken waterwheel. Outside the gates of Mapledurham lies the tiny one-street village, a calendar-photographer's dream of mellow red-brick cottages and almshouses.

Hardwick House and Stud Farm

From Mapledurham return to The White House, where a PB sign ('Whitchurch 2½ miles') points left along a track through the fields. In ½ mile (0.75km) you pass through the elaborately curlicued iron gates of Hardwick House (665776), and continue along the drive past the house itself, with glimpses over its hedge of mellow brick chimneys and gables. Pass the striking C-shaped, half-timbered stable block of Hardwick Stud Farm (654779) – if a friendly stablehand is around, you might even be allowed to stroke one of the horses, and you'll certainly see them grazing in the nearby meadows.

Pass through gates and keep ahead along a lane ('Whitchurch' sign). Soon a raised footpath on the right makes car-avoidance easier. After a mile of road walking you reach the B471 (634775); turn left through Whitchurch for ½ mile (0.75km), passing the Greyhound and the Ferryboat pubs to cross the Thames by Whitchurch Toll Bridge (636768), one of only two toll bridges still operating on the river. It's a free passage for walkers.

On the south bank bear right in 150 yards (150m) along a brick-walled alley. Keep along this narrow fenced and hedged path beside the Thames to reach the A329 opposite the entrance to Pangbourne station (632767).

If you wish to make a short Kenneth Grahame pilgrimage before catching your train, continue into the handsome Edwardian town of Pangbourne. Grahame lived in Church Cottage from 1924 until his death in 1932, and he is buried in the churchyard of St James the Less. 'The most touching thing of all,' declared a newspaper account of the writer's funeral, 'were the flowers, sent by children from all over the country, with cards attached in a childish scrawl, saying how much they loved him. The grave was lined with thousands of sweet peas, and the scent was unforgettable.' Kenneth Grahame was 'the eternal boy, keenly alive to the beauty and wonder of the world around him'.

HENLEY-ON-THAMES, GREYS COURT & ROTHERFIELD PEPPARD

A gorgeous secluded valley – a favourite haunt of red kites – sinuates west from the famous rowing town of Henley-on-Thames, taking you to two of east Oxfordshire's most attractive small villages, Rotherfield Greys and Rotherfield Peppard. There is also a chance to look over Greys Court – a historic house infused with bizarre stories. The return walk to Henley lies along ancient green lanes and trackways frequented by songbirds.

Start & Finish:	Henley-on-Thames Station
Length of walk:	8½ miles (13.5km)
OS maps:	1:50,000 Landranger 175; 1:25,000 Explorer 171
Travel:	By rail from London Paddington (55 mins); by road – M4 (Jct 10), A321; or M40 (Jct 4), A404, A4155.
Features:	Henley-on-Thames waterfront; Knollys monuments in St Nicholas's Church, Rotherfield Greys; Greys Court; Rotherfield Peppard Common; Pack and Prime Lane and Dog Lane.
Refreshments:	Maltsters Arms PH, Rotherfield Greys; Dog Inn or Red Lion PH, Rotherfield Peppard.

THE WALK

Henley-on-Thames

Henley-on-Thames has one of the most attractive waterfronts along the River Thames. The tower of the parish church looks towards the river over the roofs of the houses with their boat moorings, verandahs and riverside yards and gardens. During the Henley Royal Regatta, the crux of Henley's

Opposite: The historic Elizabethan house of Greys Court, so rich in romance and tragedy, also boasts beautiful walled gardens, which are open to the public throughout the summer months.

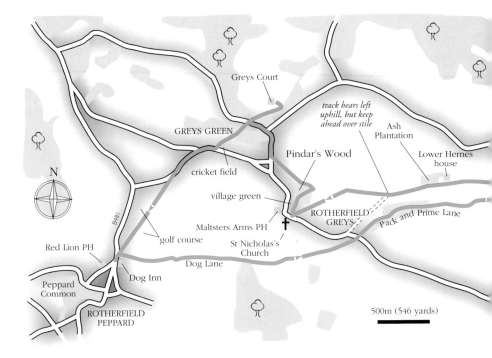

Greys Court

*track bears left
uphill, but keep
ahead over stile*   Ash
Plantation

GREYS GREEN

Pindar's Wood   Lower Hernes
house

N   cricket field

village green   ROTHERFIELD   Pack and Prime Lane
                       GREYS

B481   Maltsters Arms PH   ✝

Red Lion PH   golf course   St Nicholas's
                                    Church

Peppard   Dog Lane
Common   Dog Inn

ROTHERFIELD   500m (546 yards)
PEPPARD

summertime social calendar, the waterfront is at its most colourful and animated, but it's worth the two-minute detour from the railway station at any time of year.

From Henley-on-Thames Station (764823) walk to the Imperial Hotel. Turn right if you want to view the waterfront from Henley Bridge; otherwise turn left to cross a road and keep forward (762823 – 'Holy Trinity Church' fingerpost) up a tarmac path. Bear right by gates at the top along a walled lane to a road junction (759824). Cross over and head down Deanfield Avenue, turning immediately left along a shady path (FP fingerpost). In 350 yards (350m) join a road and keep forward, to turn right along Tilebarn Close. At the top (753822) bear left into the fields along a track between a fence and a hedge (yellow arrow on post). In ¹/₃ mile (0.5km) cross Pack and Prime Lane by a stile (748825) and keep forward on a fenced track that curves west along the valley floor.

Red kites

As soon as you leave Henley behind, the ground steepens to green grassy shoulders under fine beeches and oaks. The valley leading west curves with the soft chalk; it has a broad shallow floor between sloping sides

that rise smoothly to ridges parallel to the path. There are plantations of larch, ash, beech and fir trees, and huge specimen beeches and cedars in the valley.

This is an excellent place to spot red kites. Since the reintroduction of these dramatically beautiful birds of prey to the Chiltern Hills at the end of the 20th century – an act of conservation that redressed centuries of persecution by gamekeepers, farmers and egg-collectors – numbers have soared. Over 300 pairs were reported to be thriving in the Chilterns by the year 2000. Red kites have a russet–red back, black-lined wings and a deeply forked tail which tilts to every movement of the air. When they hover, the ends of their wings open into 'fingers' like those of a golden eagle. They seem remarkably unconcerned by the proximity of walkers, and will hover so closely overhead that you can hear their wings flap like yacht sails in a breeze.

Pass through the skirt of Ash Plantation below Lower Hernes house. In 250 yards (250m), where the track snakes a little to the left (735825) and goes uphill to the left of a belt of trees in the valley bottom, leave the track and cross a stile beside the first of the trees (yellow arrow). Continue with the hedge on your left through a gate, and in 100 yards (100m) turn left over a stile (732826 – yellow arrow) through the hedge. Turn right to cross another stile, then bear left up the slope with a fence on your left. At the crest of the hill, pass the corner of Pindar's Wood (728824) and continue across Rotherfield Greys village green to the road and church (726823).

Rotherfield Greys and the naughty Knollyses

There are fine beech trees around the village green, and a beacon complete with its fire basket. The Maltsters Arms is a pleasant pub. In the flint-built Norman church stands the imposing Knollys tomb. Sir Francis Knollys and his wife in splendid Elizabethan dress lie between marble pillars, while their son Sir William Knollys and his spouse kneel on the roof. A row of piously kneeling daughters is lined up along the tomb edge; their brothers are hidden from view on the far side of the monument.

It was Sir William's sister-in-law, Frances Howard, who really put the cat among the scandal pigeons. Beautiful and wilful, she divorced her husband the Earl of Essex and took up with Robert Carr, Earl of Somerset. When Sir Thomas Overbury, a courtier-poet and close acquaintance of Somerset's, tried to advise his friend against the liaison, the furious Frances pulled strings to have him clapped into the Tower of London, where he mysteriously died in 1613. Within a few months Frances had married Somerset, and for a time all seemed fine. But rumours began to fly. Two years later, arrested and accused of murdering Overbury, Frances admitted to having had the poet's food laced with poison. The Somersets were spared sentence of death, but imprisoned in the Tower until 1621. Then a royal order released them, on condition that they live at Greys Court and refrain from travelling more than three miles from the house.

From the church, return diagonally across the village green, aiming for a stile on the edge of Pindar's Wood. Cross it, and descend through the wood. Cross the stile at the bottom (729826) and turn left along the wood edge. Continue over stiles to a road (725828). Turn right for 250 yards (250m), then left along a side road. In 200 yards (200m) turn right (723832) up a drive to reach Greys Court (725834).

Greys Court

This very handsome late-Elizabethan manor house, where many of the Knollys/Howard shenanigans took place, stands in the courtyard of a 14th-century castle. The Great Tower, still a dominant feature, was built and crenellated by John, 1st Lord de Grey, around 1348. In the following century the castle passed to the Lovells, a family haunted by a curious fate. A Lovell bride, playing hide-and-seek at her wedding feast, became trapped in a trunk and was discovered years later, a skeleton still clothed in her wedding dress. Bizarrely, the last of the family, Francis, Viscount Lovell, is said to have met much the same end. Having rebelled against King Henry VIII, the fugitive hid from the king's search parties in the cellar after entrusting the key to a loyal servant. But this man was unluckily killed – and, as he had told no-one where his master was, the wretched Lovell starved to death behind the locked cellar door.

The interior of Greys Court is a fascinating assemblage of different architectural periods, from the massive medieval style of the kitchens through Jacobean furnishings to superb 18th-century rococo plasterwork. Outside you'll find a wheelhouse with its original wheel for raising water from the 200-foot well by donkey power, a Tudor building known as

Bachelor's Hall ('*Melius nil coelibe vita*, nothing is sweeter than the celibate life' says the inscription over the door – a slogan with plenty of relevance, given the various marital dramas played out in these surroundings), and fine gardens with some rare trees.

Return down the drive to the road. Turn right for 20 yards (20m), then go left across a stile (yellow arrow) and over the field. Climb to cross a stile into a wood, and keep ahead up through the trees to cross another stile. Aim ahead to leave the wood (721831), and follow a path to cross Greys Green cricket field and turn right along the grass verge of a road. Pass a side-turning on your right (718830); in another 400 yards (400m) turn left off the road through a gate (715827 – FP fingerpost). Cross a rough stretch of land and a tree plantation through the middle of a golf course for ½ mile (0.75km) to reach the B481 at the Dog Inn in Rotherfield Peppard (710820).

Rotherfield Peppard Common

'Rotherfield' means 'the clearing of the hryther', 'hryther' being a Saxon word for cattle. Stone Age and Bronze Age tribes from the Thames Valley ventured into these uplands to collect the flints they lacked in their gravelly lowlands, but it was the people of the Dark Ages who made major inroads into the Chiltern wildwood for grazing purposes. Peppard Common, just across the B481, is 56 acres (23ha) of carefully preserved common land, a remnant of open grazing that was cleared of trees centuries ago by axe and fire.

Dog Lane and Pack and Prime Lane

Long stretches of green lane – under the name of Dog Lane, followed by Pack and Prime Lane – lead from Rotherfield Peppard back towards Henley. Dog Lane is more like 'Bog Lane' in parts, running stickily between high hedges of blackthorn, hazel and field maple. In Pack and Prime Lane you may see and hear warblers, long-tailed tits, goldcrests and woodpeckers among the surrounding holly bushes and oak, ash and horse chestnut trees. This is a centuries-old trade and droving route delightful to idle along.

From Rotherfield Peppard follow Dog Lane up the left side of the Dog Inn ('Right Of Way' fingerpost and 'Single Track Road' notice), and on for ⅔ mile (1km). At a tarmac lane (723819) keep ahead for ⅓ mile (0.5km) to pass two houses on your right. Immediately after, turn right over a stile (728820 – double fingerpost); follow the left-hand of the two paths indicated, to cross the left-hand of two stiles in a fence. Aim well to the right of a house ahead, following the path to cross a stile and go over a road (733821 – FP fingerpost). Follow the bridleway along Pack and Prime Lane for a mile (1.6km) to a stile (748825); turn right here, and retrace your steps to Henley Station.

GREAT MISSENDEN, HUGHENDEN & HIGH WYCOMBE

This beautiful walk, through Chiltern beech-woods and over Buckinghamshire farmland and downland slopes, runs south from the valley of the River Misbourne at Great Missenden. There are long stretches (sometimes very muddy) through mixed woodland as you drop down into the well-manicured and charming Hughenden Valley. The shadow of Benjamin Disraeli, twice Prime Minister at the height of the Victorian era, lies long hereabouts. Hughenden Manor was his home, and the statesman himself is buried by the wall of St Michael and All Angels' Church in Hughenden. The walk ends with a long descent down a 'secret' lane into the heart of High Wycombe.

Start:	Great Missenden Station
Finish:	High Wycombe Station
Length of walk:	9 miles (14km)
OS maps:	1:50,000 Landranger 175; 1:25,000 Explorers 181, 172
Travel:	By rail from London Marylebone (40 mins); by road – M40 (Jct 1), A413.
Features:	Lovely woods and lanes; beautiful Hughenden Valley; Disraeli and other memorials in the Church of St Michael and All Angels, Hughenden; Hughenden Manor.
Refreshments:	Polecat Inn on the A4128 south of Prestwood; White Lion PH, Cryers Hill; restaurant and tea-room at Hughenden Manor.

THE WALK

Mischievous monks of Missenden
Great Missenden is a typically neat and well-looked-after Chiltern commuter village these days, but in pre-Reformation days the Augustinian

monks of Missenden Abbey seem to have enjoyed some high old times. Scandal and the monks were bedfellows on more than one occasion. In 1297, one of the novices cut his own throat rather than face the rigours of monastic life at Missenden; but discipline must have slackened over the next half century, for during King Edward III's reign one of the monastery's abbots was hanged for clipping coins (the criminal practice of clipping small segments out of the rim of silver or gold coins, and making new coins out of the stolen shavings). By the time of the Reformation, the Missenden monks had become all but indistinguishable from ordinary villagers. One of the monks was spotted, according to local report, lurching 'at midnight out of a house in the village in doublet and jerkin, with a sword by his side'. However, the Missenden monks were useful to the local community as physicians, prescribing such cures as marrowbone of horses and oil of black snails.

From the station platform (893013) climb steps from the London platform to the road and hairpin immediately back to your left down Trafford Road. In 300 yards (300m) turn right up the side of Station View Cottages (893011 – Chiltern Heritage Trail sign and FP fingerpost). Cross a stile, walk diagonally left across a field to another stile, which you cross to join a footpath running along the back of the cottage gardens, then turn right (PB fingerpost) up a tarmac lane. Be careful not to take the fenced footpath on the left of the lane, as this diverges after 200 yards (200m).

View over Great Missenden
At the top of the hill, pause to admire the view back over the church tower and the roofs of Great Missenden peeping out of the trees in the Misbourne Valley, with the slope of the valley rising beyond to a wooded ridge.

The lane levels out at the top of the hill. Bear left to pass in front of View Farm (889007), and keep ahead along a tree-shaded bridleway. In 200 yards (200m) it swings right; in another 100 yards (100m), ignore a footpath stile on your right (887005). Continue along the bridleway for another 150 yards (150m) to where it swings left. Cross a stile on your right at this bend (886005 – yellow blob waymark) and follow the path along the lower edge of Atkins Wood. In 350 yards (350m) leave the wood and bear left (yellow arrow on post), keeping ahead for 300 yards (300m) to cross a stile onto the road (880001). Bear right for 10 yards (10m), then left down Church Path (PB fingerpost). Where the houses end, the bridleway keeps ahead; bear left off the bridleway here (879000 – FP fingerpost) to go southwards through Peterley Wood, following Chiltern Society white arrows painted on trees.

At the far edge of the wood you meet a bridleway (878996) at a post with a blue 'PB' arrow pointing right and a yellow 'FP' arrow pointing left. Turn left here, following painted white arrows for 200 yards (200m) to reach a post. A blue 'PB' arrow points on ahead, but turn right here (yellow FP arrow) over a stile to leave the wood. Follow a fenced path to cross the A4128 at the Polecat Inn (876994). Walk down the right side of the pub (FP fingerpost); continue along a field edge and over a stile, then on across the next field down to a stile (872992) where you turn left along the road. In 150 yards (150m) turn right (FP fingerpost) on a path through Longfield Wood.

Peterley Wood and Longfield Wood

Peterley Wood, just back along the way, was an uncultivated wasteland until the monks of Missenden Abbey hedged and ditched it in the late 12th century. Old beeches and tangles of holly grow on the level ground of what must have been common grazing, and you can still make out the shapes of the monks' earth banks and ditches. Longfield Wood, by contrast, is long and thin – a slender strip of mixed woodland a mile (1.6km) long but only 100 yards (100m) wide for most of its length – and curves along the crest and sides of the steep valley whose contours it clings to like a second skin.

It's not hard to get lost in Longfield Wood, so keep your eyes open! The path forks among holly bushes 350 yards (350m) after entering the wood; one branch slants uphill to the left, but be sure to take the branch that slopes down to the right. Pass under power cables (869988), then in 300 yards (300m) cross two stiles. In ¼ mile (0.4km) you reach a post (867983), here a permissive path keeps straight ahead, but you follow the path to the left. In another ¼ mile (0.4km) you join a tarmac drive and continue forward to a road (870980) where you turn right.

In ⅓ mile (0.5km) turn left over a stile (866980 – FP fingerpost) and climb the hillside. Cross a stile at the top and keep forward to the corner of a wood (866976 – stile and Buckinghamshire County Council yellow arrow), where you turn left along the wood edge. Cross a stile (yellow arrow) and another stile after a further 50 yards (50m), and continue across a field. In 150 yards (150m) turn right over a stile and cross a school drive (870976). Go down a fenced path and over a stile to cross another drive and go through an iron kissing gate (FP fingerpost). Continue over a field to cross a stile to pick up a path with a barbed wire fence running along the left, on the eastern flank of Gomms Wood. In 80 yards (80m) emerge and keep ahead with a hedge on your left. At the far end of this

Opposite: Benjamin Disraeli bought 18th-century Hughenden Manor in 1847. He and his wife, Mary Anne, Viscountess Beaconsfield, adored the house and its gardens, woods and fields – a retreat from the hurly-burly of political London.

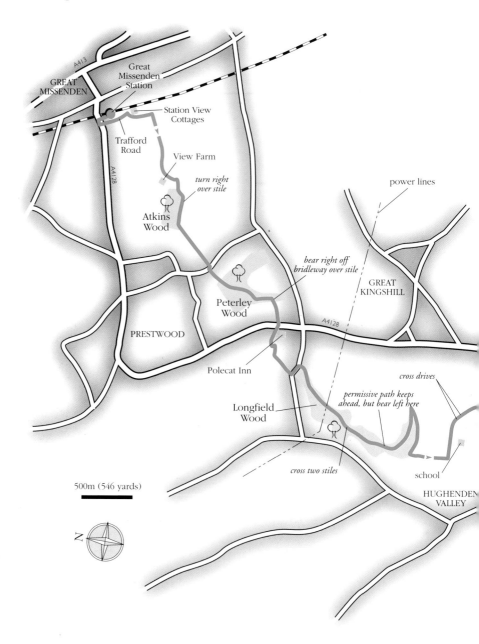

GREAT MISSENDEN

A413

Great Missenden Station

Station View Cottages

Trafford Road

A4128

View Farm

turn right over stile

Atkins Wood

power lines

bear right off bridleway over stile

GREAT KINGSHILL

Peterley Wood

PRESTWOOD

A4128

Polecat Inn

cross drives

permissive path keeps ahead, but bear left here

Longfield Wood

cross two stiles

school

HUGHENDEN VALLEY

500m (546 yards)

N

WIDMER
END

CRYERS
HILL

White Lion PH

turn sharp right onto
a green lane

'secret'
lane

HIGH
WYCOMBE

barn

High Wycombe
Station

Gomms
Wood

A4128

Green
Hill Road

The
Greenway

Church of
St Michael
and All
Angels

small lake

A40

Hughenden
Manor

field join a fenced path to reach the A4128 at Cryers Hill (875969). Just to your left are a post office/shop and the White Lion pub.

Turn right along the A4128 for 100 yards (100m), then cross the road and follow a path through the trees (FP fingerpost). Kissing gates and yellow arrows bring you along field edges and then through trees. In ¼ mile (0.4km) pass two gates on your right, and keep ahead along the top edge of a wood and then a green lane. At a stile (869960) dogleg right, then left along a field edge with a hedge on your right. Pass a barn (868958), and at the next hedge turn right (stile and blue arrow) to the A4128 (867955). Cross the road (with great care!) and turn left for 50 yards (50m), then turn right up the drive to St Michael and All Angels' Church (864955).

The Disraelis and Hughenden

The Hughenden Valley is a rural Home Counties idyll, so neat and beautiful are its grassy meadows and well-kept woodlands, especially the 560 acres (225ha) of the Hughenden Estate owned and cared for by the National Trust. Benjamin Disraeli – leader of the Tory party, twice Prime Minister of Great Britain, successful novelist and incorrigible romantic – bought the estate in 1847 and grew to love it passionately during the 25 years he spent here with his wife Mary Anne, Viscountess Beaconsfield. The Disraelis were hands-on owners; they landscaped and planted the gardens and many of the woodlands, built a splendid set of stables (these now house the National Trust's ticket office, shop and tea-rooms), and from 1862 remodelled the plain Georgian house of Hughenden Manor in dashing Gothic style. Disraeli made sure that a pinch of drama attended life at Hughenden – he armed the servants with revolvers to counter burglarious attempts, installed a flock of peacocks to amuse Mary Anne, and appointed a little lad to the post of 'peacock-ward'.

A tour of Hughenden Manor brings the Disraelis to life with many personal touches – pictures of their special friends, testimonials and presentation objects, Gothic furniture made for Disraeli, his books and writing materials, along with portraits of Queen Victoria. The queen had a special soft spot for 'Dizzy'. In the Church of St Michael and All Angels is the personal memorial she dedicated: 'To the dear and honoured memory of Benjamin Earl of Beaconsfield, this memorial is placed by his grateful Sovereign and friend, Victoria R.I. – "Kings loveth him that speaketh right", Proverbs XVI, 13. February 27 1882'. Benjamin and Mary Anne lie outside the east end of the church, together with Disraeli's brothers and nephew, and a female fan who had begged to be buried beside her hero. There are many other treasures in the church – they include very fine Victorian stained glass, a beautiful early Norman tub font with floral carving, and a calm and blissful Arts and Crafts mural of the Adoration. There is also a curious collection of Tudor forgeries of 13th- and 14th-century knightly tomb effigies; these were installed during the reign of King Henry VIII by local squire George Wellesbourne, in order to give himself a grand set of 'ancestors' and bolster his spurious claim to be descended from the noble De Montfort family.

After visiting Hughenden Manor (861953) return down the drive to the cattle grid above the church (863955). Turn right here and walk south through the park along the valley side, aiming to go through a kissing gate halfway down the fence ahead. From here the path drops gradually down the slope to go through the next kissing gate just above a small lake (863949). The stream soon bends away left, but keep ahead to a road (864944), where you turn left to cross the A4128 (866943). Climb Green Hill Road through a long S-bend. In ½ mile (0.75km), where the road bends sharp right opposite Brands Hill Avenue at the top of the hill, turn even sharper right (872946 – FP fingerpost) through beech trees to follow a green lane.

'Secret' lane into High Wycombe

This is a fine way to enter High Wycombe, nearly a mile of 'secret' lane which drops south along the valley side into the very centre of the town, hedged and fenced all the way; a lane too narrow for cars, but well used by townspeople on foot.

In 350 yards (350m), as the green lane begins to dip steeply downhill, bear left (871943) on a rising track that soon crosses a road (871942). Keep forward along the lane ('No bicycles' notice), descending for ½ mile (0.75km) to cross a road (868933). Keep ahead down The Greenway; turn left at the bottom to cross the A404 (868931), and continue for 250 yards (250m). Turn right down Albert Street and walk through Duke Street car-park to enter High Wycombe Station (870930). If this entrance barrier is closed, cross under the railway through the underpass and turn right to reach the front of the station.

BERKHAMSTED COMMON, ASHRIDGE HOUSE & FRITHSDEN BEECHES

When 19th-century noble landowners wanted something, they generally got their way. But Lord Brownlow of Ashridge bit off more than he could chew when he decided to enclose Berkhamsted Common in 1866. The full saga of how he was defeated, and the common saved for public enjoyment, unfolds as you cross this open land above Berkhamsted and take a look at Brownlow's grand mansion, Ashridge House. The return walk brings you among the ancient pollarded trees of Frithsden Beeches, a very rare fragment of a medieval wood pasture.

Start & Finish:	Berkhamsted Station
Length of walk:	6½ miles (10.5km)
OS maps:	1:50,000 Landrangers 165, 166; 1:25,000 Explorer 181
Travel:	By rail from London Euston (35 mins); by road – M25 (Jct 20), A41, A416 or A4251.
Features:	Berkhamsted Castle; Berkhamsted Common; Ashridge House; Frithsden Beeches.
Refreshments:	Many pubs and cafés in Berkhamsted.

THE WALK

To view narrowboats negotiating the locks of the tree-hung Grand Union Canal, turn right out of Berkhamsted Station (993082) and the canal bridge is 200 yards (200m) along the road. Return past the station and under the railway line. Berkhamsted Castle (995082) is 50 yards (50m) on your right.

Opposite: Beech woods are characteristic of the chalky Chiltern ridges, and the shady paths that run through Berkhamsted Common show off Frithsden Beeches beautifully.

Berkhamsted Castle

This is a site with a special place in British history. Berkhamsted Castle was one of the first to be built after the Norman Conquest. Count Robert Mortmain, William the Conqueror's half brother, began work on a wooden castle beside the River Bulbourne immediately after the victory at Hastings. It was here, in November 1066, that William received the homage of those Saxon nobles who had survived the battle, and gave orders to Bishop Ealdred to prepare to crown him King at Westminster Abbey on the forthcoming Christmas Day.

The castle was rebuilt in flint and stone in the mid-12th century, and was a royal residence until Tudor times. It's this early medieval stonework that you see today; a big oval of broken flint curtain wall, some of its standing up to 20 feet (6m) high, encircling the broad platform of the outer ward, with the green grassy thumb of the inner ward's mound sticking up at the north-east corner. To the south, the railway runs through the outer earthworks and moat, having carried away the main gateway and its defensive barbican during construction – they wouldn't get away with it today!

Return from the castle to the mini-roundabout to the right of the railway bridge, and turn right along Brownlow Road. In 100 yards (100m) the road bends right, keep ahead up Castle Hill for 50 yards (50m). At the left bend keep ahead across a stile (994084 – 'Berkhamsted Common 1' FP fingerpost and yellow arrow) through Berkhamsted Collegiate School's sports field car-park. At the end of the tarmac continue along a grassy track; cross a stile, and shortly turn left through a kissing gate (996088 – FP fingerpost). Please note that OS Explorer 181 shows the footpath on the right side of the hedge, but in fact it runs on the left.

From the next kissing gate continue up the slope of the hill with the hedge on your right. At the top of the slope, cross a stile and continue straight along a field track, keeping the hedge on your left. The track soon bends left (993094) to run north-west with a hedge on the left. Pass through the hedge at the far end of the field and turn right (991097 – post with 3 yellow arrows), heading north-north-east past an old pond among bushes, with a hedge on your right. Drop down two fields to cross a stile in the dip and climb to cross a stile into the woods (993102).

Keep straight ahead on a narrow track through the trees for 150 yards (150m), then turn left along a bridleway (post with blue PB arrows). In 300 yards (300m) you join the track from Brickkiln Cottage, seen to your right among the trees. Keep ahead to reach the edge of the trees at gates (992104); don't go through the gates, but continue to follow the path along the inside edge of the wood. In 300 yards (300m) the path bears right

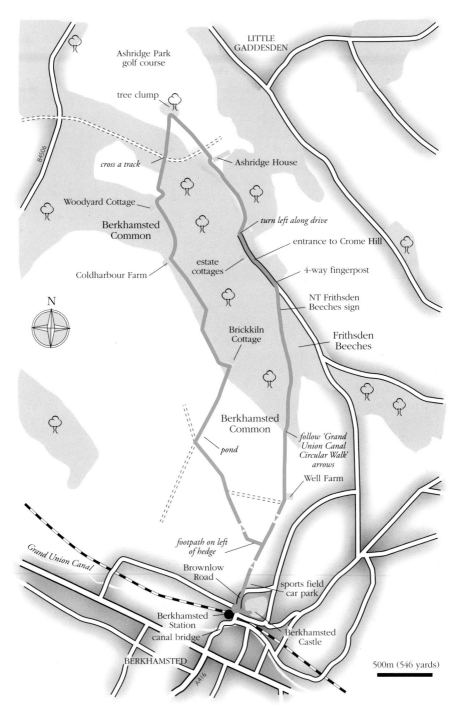

LITTLE
GADDESDEN

Ashridge Park
golf course

tree clump

cross a track

Ashridge House

B4506

Woodyard Cottage

Berkhamsted
Common

turn left along drive

entrance to Crome Hill

estate
cottages

4-way fingerpost

Coldharbour Farm

NT Frithsden
Beeches sign

N

Frithsden
Beeches

Brickkiln
Cottage

Berkhamsted
Common

*follow 'Grand
Union Canal
Circular Walk'
arrows*

pond

Well Farm

*footpath on left
of hedge*

Grand Union Canal

Brownlow
Road

sports field
car park

Berkhamsted
Station

canal bridge

Berkhamsted
Castle

BERKHAMSTED

A416

500m (546 yards)

37

(991107) through the wood and meets a bridleway at the northern edge (992108 – post and blue arrows). Turn left here inside the rim of the wood, with open ground on your right. In 300 yards (300m) the path continues ahead deeper into the wood (991110). In 150 yards (150m), keep ahead at a post ('Ashridge Estate Boundary Trail' arrow, '47' marker and blue arrow) to bear right opposite Coldharbour Farm (989113 – posts with blue arrows) on a curving forest road across a wooded sector of Berkhamsted Common.

The Battle of Berkhamsted Common

The long tract of open and wooded country along the ridge north of Berkhamsted is a remnant of what was once an enormous common wood called The Frith – 'a wood for a thousand swine' records the Domesday Book. The Frith was a forest where the locals grazed their cattle and cut bracken for fuel and bedding. At prescribed intervals the bounds would be ceremonially beaten and boys bumped at important points to ensure the next generation remembered just where the common's boundaries lay. Berkhamsted residents took for granted their right to roam on the common until 1866, when Lord Brownlow of the adjacent Ashridge Estate arbitrarily enclosed one third of the ground inside iron fences with no gates or means of access. He had offered the townsfolk 43 acres (17ha) of land in Berkhamsted for a recreation ground in exchange for their rights of commonage, and most had agreed, Esau-like, to take this mess of pottage in exchange for their birthrights. But local property-owner Augustus Smith was determined not to let the peer have his way.

Ironically, Smith himself was a fabulously autocratic landowner who had bought the Scilly Isles and ran them with a rigid rod of iron. But Brownlow's arrogance had got his goat. With the bit of righteousness between his teeth, Smith went into action to rescue Berkhamsted Common from the noble lord's clutches. He organised and paid a gang of navvies to come down from London and remove the iron railings by force. A special train left Euston Station just after midnight, carrying 100 selected men armed with hammers, chisels and crowbars. The two contractors who had engaged them had got blind drunk in a pub near Euston, but a clear-headed lawyer's clerk coordinated the men when they disembarked at Tring station and marched them up to the common. *Punch* magazine, a fortnight after the event, set the scene:

> Spoke out their nameless leader,
> 'That railing must go down.'
> Then firmer grasped the crowbar
> Those hands so strong and brown.

> They march against the railing,
> They lay the crowbars low,
> And down and down for many a yard
> The costly railings go.

Before first light the men had knocked down three miles of iron railings that had cost Lord Brownlow £1,000 to erect. The railings were neatly rolled up and left for the Ashridge estate workers to collect. In the morning the locals came flocking on foot and in carriages, gigs and dogcarts to stroll across the common. Many took away sprigs of gorse as tokens that the land was theirs again.

The National Trust owns most of the common now, and people are free to walk where they will (although certain areas, such as Frithsden Beeches – see below – need to be treated with sensitivity). The Battle of Berkhamsted Common, and other contemporary attempts to enclose Wimbledon Common and Hampstead Heath, had long-term repercussions, leading to the formation of the Commons, Open Spaces and Footpaths Preservation Society, and to a general appreciation of the necessity to preserve such precious open spaces. As *Punch* summed it all up:

> Bold was the deed and English
> The Commoners have done,
> Let's hope the law of England, too,
> Will smile upon their fun.
> For our few remaining Commons
> Must not be seized or sold,
> Nor Lords forget they do not live
> In the bad days of old.

By Woodyard Cottage (987117) follow the track round a right bend; then turn left over a stile (yellow arrow). Cross the field northwards to cross a stile into a wood (988120). Keep ahead, following white arrows on tree trunks. In 150 yards (150m) cross a track (yellow arrow and 'No Horses' notice). Continue ahead, following white arrows, to leave the wood on the edge of Ashridge Park golf course (989124). Head due north across the fairway to a tree clump, then turn right and follow the edge of the wood to a yellow arrow on a post at the corner of a wood. This arrow points forward through the trees. In 150 yards (150m) leave the trees, with Ashridge House (994122) dead ahead.

Ashridge House

This enormous and imposing mansion (now a college) stands on a monastic site and was remodelled by James Wyatt for the 7th Earl of Bridgewater in 1808 as a Gothic extravaganza. Turrets, chapel spire, battlements and other embellishments reflect the family's wealth, power and prestige – as does the sheer size of the frontage, which is a mighty 1,000 feet (300m) wide. From the edge of the trees you can look back west, along a straight avenue 1½ miles (2.5km) long, to see the tall obelisk of the Bridgewater Monument, which was erected in 1832 in memory of the 3rd Duke of Bridgewater, a formidable promoter and builder of canals.

Aim for the right side of Ashridge House to cross a road and turn right (FP fingerpost) along a fence and hedge. In 70 yards (70m) turn left (991121 – yellow arrow) along Ashridge House's boundary fence. Shortly after the buildings end, bear slightly right away from the fence to turn left along the college's drive (995115) for some distance. Pass estate cottages on the right and the entrance to Crome Hill on the left. In 300 yards (300m) you come to a four-way fingerpost on your left (998110). Two of its 'PB' signs point into the woods on the right of the road. Follow the left-hand of these, slanting uphill for 200 yards (200m), to leave the trees and bear left along the wood edge. In 150 yards (150m), at a 'NT Frithsden Beeches' sign (998108), join a track along the upper edge of the wood. In 200 yards (200m), where the wood edge curves to the right, keep ahead (PB fingerpost) through the woodland of Frithsden Beeches.

Frithsden Beeches

These ancient beech-woods, the remains of a medieval wood pasture, were acquired by the National Trust in 1925 after the Ashridge Estate had decided to fell them. The oldest beeches are pollards – gnarled trees whose limbs have been periodically cut back over the centuries to give clearance for animals to graze; some could be 250 years old or more. Although the public has unrestricted access to Frithsden Beeches, the NT appreciates it if you keep to the paths in order not to disturb the wildlife of these woods.

Soon you dip into a dell (blue arrows on a post). Keep ahead, up the slope and on, to leave the trees (999103) and continue south across the scrubland of Berkhamsted Common, crossing several bridleways. Where the scrub trees end, follow 'Grand Union Canal Circular Walk' arrows on posts down a grassy slope and through another belt of woodland. At the bottom edge of the trees, cross a stile (998097) and bear left along a field edge to cross a stile into a hedged, grassy lane. It leads south for ⅓ mile (0.5km) to Well Farm. Cross a stile at the farm (998092) and follow the field edge back to Berkhamsted.

HARLINGTON, BUNYAN'S OAK & SHARPENHOE CLAPPERS

The Chiltern Hills, officially at their northernmost outpost on the outer slope of the Dunstable Downs, own a curious detached enclave several miles further north, the sinuously curving chalk rampart of the Sundon Hills. This is the final step down from the 750-foot (230-m) heights of the Chilterns to the Bedfordshire plains some 500 feet (150m) below. The walk begins at Harlington, on the edge of Bedfordshire's lowland country of heavy clay, and works its way round to climb to the crest of the hills for an exhilarating ridge tramp with marvellous chalk downland flowers in spring and summer, and spectacular views at any time of year.

Start & Finish:	Harlington Station
Length of walk:	8 miles (13km)
OS maps:	1:50,000 Landranger 166; 1:25,000 Explorer 193
Travel:	By rail from London King's Cross (45 mins); by road – M1 (Jct 12), A5120 for ¹/₂ mile (0.75km), minor road to Harlington.
Features:	Bunyan's Oak; green lane from Upper Sampshill Farm; Sharpenhoe Clappers; Sundon Hills.
Refreshments:	The Lynmore PH, Sharpenhoe.

THE WALK

From Harlington Station (035303) turn right to cross the railway and keep ahead to cross Sundon Road by the war memorial. Continue past the church and on along Barton Road. In ²/₃ mile (1km), just after a PB fingerpost on the right, the road bends left. Pass the side road to the left (044308 – 'Westoning, Toddington' sign) and continue along Sharpenhoe Road. In 70 yards (70m) bear left on a footpath (FP fingerpost) through the trees. In 50 yards (50m) cross a stile into a field and turn right along the hedge (FP fingerpost). In 30 yards (30m) follow the 'Public Footpath Pulloxhill 2½' FP sign across the field, aiming for a water tower on the skyline. In the valley bottom, cross a stile to the right of a spinney. Bunyan's Oak (046313) is up the slope to your left in the next field.

Bunyan's Oak and the great parable-spinner

Bunyan's Oak is dead, but still enormously impressive: a gnarled, bifurcated, grey skeleton alone on a rise of ground, its knotty limbs spreading outwards and skywards. Bark flakes off it like saurian hide. It commands a superb view across the fields to Sharpenhoe Clappers, a high chalk spur at the north-east extremity of the Sundon Hills. John Bunyan is said to have based the Delectable Mountains in *The Pilgrim's Progress* on these hills, and the view is certainly an inspiring one.

A notice fixed to the dead tree reads: 'This tree is reputed to be the oak where John Bunyan was preaching shortly before his arrest in 1660. He was later taken to Harlington Manor for interrogation.'

The magistrate, Francis Wingate JP, committed Bunyan to Bedford jail, and the preacher was shut up there for the next 12 years. In that nervous era, with widespread fear and loathing of the new nonconformist religions and their practitioners, prison was an inevitable destination for the Bedfordshire tinker's son with his inextinguishable missionary zeal and his fierce independence of mind.

John Bunyan had not been an especially religious-minded youth. Born in 1628 in the village of Elstow just south of Bedford, he followed his father's trade, and loved to sing, dance and play his fiddle. He married a local girl and had four children. But in his twenties Bunyan began to be troubled by deep upheavals of the spirit. John Gifford, a pioneer of the Independent religious movement, inspired him to preach and to write – Bunyan's first book was a demolition of the tenets of another new branch of faith, Quakerism.

His first long spell in jail gave Bunyan the leisure to write several religious tracts. In 1672 there was a Declaration of Indulgence and a slackening of official persecution of nonconformist sects. Bunyan was released, and took up a full-time calling as a licensed Independent preacher. But four years later the Declaration was revoked and he landed back in prison – only for six months, but during this time he wrote the first part of *The Pilgrim's Progress*. The Delectable Mountains were often in sight

Opposite: From the high ridge of the Sundon Hills you look out on tremendous views to all points of the compass. Sharpenhoe Clappers is one of Bedfordshire's most popular beauty spots.

of Christian, the fable's hero, during his dangerous journey from the City of Destruction to the Celestial City, and Bunyan in his prison cell must frequently have had this view of the Sundon Hills in mind as he wrote.

The Pilgrim's Progress was published in 1678, with a sequel in 1685. By that time Bunyan had taken to a wandering life as an itinerant preacher. After riding through a rainstorm in August 1688 he caught a chill, and died soon afterwards.

The great parable-spinner would be pleased to see that his namesake oak shelters a small living elder tree; while in front of the dead giant grows a slender oak sapling, planted by Dr David Bellamy in July 1988 to commemorate the tercentenary of John Bunyan's death.

Go through the gate at the bottom of Bunyan's Oak field (black arrow in a yellow circle). At the end of the next field cross a stile (black arrow) and a footbridge to go forward with a landfill site behind a hedge on your right. At a post with arrows (049315) steer diagonally left across a wide field, aiming for Upper Sampshill Farm on its ridge ahead. Skirt the angle of a hedge (050318), and cross two stiles in quick succession (black arrows) to walk uphill with a hedge on your right. At the top of the slope, beside Upper Sampshill Farm, pass a blocked gate on your right; in another 15 yards (15m) turn right through gates (051321) and right again along the farm track. In 10 yards (10m) bear right down a green lane (notice: 'Cars & Motorbikes prohibited, October–April inclusive'), and follow this lane for ⅔ mile (1km) to Harlington Road at Mill Farm (053313). This is a beautiful, grassy green lane between thick hedges, an ancient route through the fields.

John Bunyan Trail

Turn left along the road past Harlington Mills, round a nasty sharp bend (please listen out for traffic and take care!) and on for 50 yards (50m). Just past Grange Farm, turn left (PB fingerpost) off the road. Aim diagonally right across rough ground towards a gap in the hedge (058312), which you pass through. Aim across the next field for a post at the left corner of Sharpenhoe Grove (060313). A black arrow points ahead beside the wood to a footbridge; turn right here (062313 – blue arrows) along the John Bunyan Trail (BT), past Bury Farm farmyard and up the farm drive to reach the road in Sharpenhoe (064306).

Turn left here past The Lynmore pub for 150 yards (150m); then turn right (FP fingerpost) up the rounded prow of Sharpenhoe Clappers. A short steep climb up steps through the trees puts you quickly at the top (066303), where the BT turns right along the path at the escarpment edge.

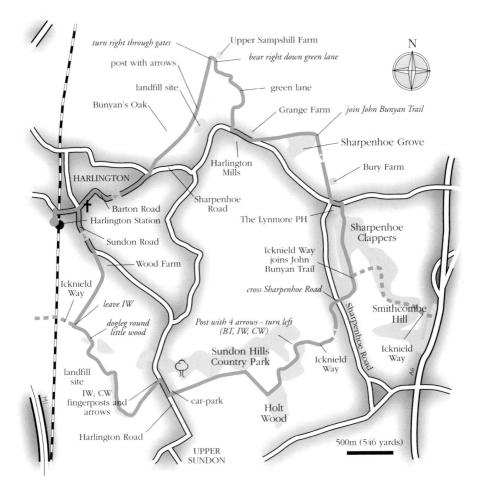

Sharpenhoe Clappers

Looking from east to west there are three sections to this wriggling 6-mile (10-km) ribbon of chalk escarpment – Smithcombe Hill, Sharpenhoe Clappers and the Sundon Hills. The beech hanger on top of Sharpenhoe Clappers was not planted until the 19th century, so John Bunyan would have known the hills as bald, grassy sheep walks. An Iron Age fort clings to the spur, its ditch running across the path in the upper skirt of the wood. The National Trust looks after clearance of hawthorn and elder scrub on the steep escarpment slope, opening up the ground for a summer chalk grassland flora that includes rock rose, horseshoe vetch, milkwort, dwarf thistle and fairy flax. The view to the north over many miles of low-lying country is wonderful.

In ⅓ mile (0.5km) a Chiltern Society waymark arrow points to the right; but keep ahead on a clear track among scrub bushes, then along the right-hand edge of an open grassy area on the nape of the downs. A yellow arrow on a gatepost announces that the BT now shares its course with the ancient Icknield Way trackway. Cross Sharpenhoe Road (065296) and keep ahead (Icknield Way/IW and Chiltern Way/CW fingerposts). Cross the next stile and bear left (CW arrow), following CW signs and black arrows. In the woods, ½ mile (0.75km) after crossing Sharpenhoe Road, you reach a post with four arrows (061291). Turn left here, following three arrows – BT, IW, CW. Now follow IW waymarks zigzagging along the wood edge for ½ mile (0.75km).

At the west corner of Holt Wood (058285), turn right (arrows on a post). Keep the hedge on your right for 300 yards (300m) to go through a kissing gate (056287) and on down a track. In another 150 yards (150m) turn left at a gate (BT, IW, CW waymarks), and keep ahead with a hedge on your left for ½ mile (0.75km).

Sundon Hills Country Park

Looking north over the wooded escarpment of the Sundon Hills there are views across 20 or 30 miles (50km) of country. The 93-acre (38-ha) country park comprises native ash woodland, patches of hazel and elder scrub with wayfaring trees, areas of grazed downland and abandoned chalk quarries. Yellowhammers, willow warblers and whitethroats sing in the scrub, and on the downland slopes grow common spotted orchid, basil and thyme, restharrow and kidney vetch, salad burnet and woolly thistle. The backs of these hills are rolling billowy downland, breezy and sunny – beautiful walking from end to end.

At a Sundon Hills Country Park car-park (047286), turn right along Harlington Road for 200 yards (200m), then left (IW, CW fingerposts and arrows) along a field edge with a hedge on your left. At the top of the field bear right (043283), soon crossing into the fringe of woodland to continue a clockwise circuit of the sloping valley. At the bottom (north-west) corner (041287) emerge from the trees and bear left, then right along the right edge of a landfill site. Dogleg round a little wood (039290), and in 300 yards (300m) leave the IW (037292), turning right with a hedge on your left towards Wood Farm. In ⅓ mile (0.6km), beside the farm, turn left over a stile (040297 – black arrow), making for the nearer end of a conifer hedge. Go over a stile here (black arrow), and follow arrows over stiles and gates across three paddocks to the road (038301). Turn left to reach Harlington Station.

WATTON-AT-STONE, BENINGTON LORDSHIP & SACOMBE

Rural Hertfordshire is the backdrop to this walk: flinty fields under enormous upland skies, fine oak woods and farms perched on ridges. St Peter's Church at Benington boasts a wonderful collection of masonry oddities and two sumptuous medieval tombs, while there are lovely seasonal gardens at Benington Lordship, not to mention an overblown 1830s folly of a mock-Norman gatehouse. Other churches at Little Munden, Sacombe and Watton-at-Stone are worth looking round (for access, see Further Information, pages 192–201). The long approach drive, extensive parkland and grand gatehouse of Woodhall Park recall an 18th-century era when entrepreneurs glutted with money made in India would lay out magnificent estates to their own greater glory.

Start & Finish:	Watton-at-Stone Station
Length of walk:	12 miles (19km)
OS maps:	1:50,000 Landranger 166; 1:25,000 Explorer 182, 193, 194
Travel:	By rail from London King's Cross (45–50 mins); by road – M25 (Jct 23), A10 (Jct 6), A1000, then minor roads by Digswell and Burham Green.
Features:	St Peter's Church, Benington; Benington Lordship; Sacombe Park; Woodhall Park; All Saints' Church, Little Munden; St Catherine's Church, Sacombe; St Andrew and St Mary's Church, Watton-at-Stone.
Refreshments:	George and Dragon PH, Watton-at-Stone; Bell Inn, Benington; Boot Free House, Dane End.

THE WALK

From Watton-at-Stone Station (296192), bear left to cross the railway and continue along the road into Watton-at-Stone to reach the village street at a mini-roundabout beside the ornate late Victorian village pump (300194).

Bear left along the village street; in 40 yards (40m) turn right down Mill Lane to cross the River Beane. In 70 yards (70m) follow the right-hand finger of a double fingerpost ('PB Blue Hill ½'), keeping a hedge on your left, along field edges for ½ mile (0.75km) to meet the A602 (298201 – blue arrow on post). Turn left in bushes for 50 yards (50m), then right (blue arrows on post) to cross the road (take great care!). A PB fingerpost on the far side points ahead. Keep a hedge on your left and follow the field edge to a gap in the far hedge where you cross a farm track and keep ahead. In 350 yards (350m), where a hedge comes down the slope to your right, turn left (299210 – blue arrow) up the middle of the field to turn right along a road. In 500 yards (500m), on a right bend, bear left (297216 – BW fingerpost) along Cotton Lane, a sunken lane and field track, for 1 mile (1.6km). In the bottom of a dip, by a little brick pump house, turn left (296228) to reach a road (295232), where you turn right into Benington. At Church Green bear left to reach St Peter's Church (297236).

St Peter's Church, Benington

St Peter's is built of knapped (cut) flint, and possesses a tremendous array of carved stone medieval heads, inside and out. There's a weather-beaten statue over the porch, and in the porch's east window two beautiful stained-glass lights: one with daffodils and a gardener's spade and fork commemorating William Eustace Mills (1881–1957), for 25 years rector of Benington; and the other with snowdrops and a painter's palette, brushes and easel in memory of the long-lived Everilda Louise Tindall Mills (1889–1992). Inside are memorial tombs to medieval knights and their ladies, and more intriguing carved figures, several in exotic headgear. Supporting the chancel arch are two Green Men of contrasting type; nearby there's an imp literally pulling a face. The elaborate ogee arch over the memorial tomb in the chancel carries a couple of gurning heads, and on the reverse a contorted likeness of a king trying to pluck a sword out of his guts. Some say this is King Edward II, depicted as suffering a death far more dignified than the horrors that were actually inflicted on him with a red-hot poker in Berkeley Castle.

In the vestry under the tower hangs a framed Proclamation of 1860 'for the Encouragement of Piety and Virtue, and for the preventing and punishing of Vice, Profaneness, and Immorality' – a fascinating document, revealing plenty about Victorian attitudes and aspirations.

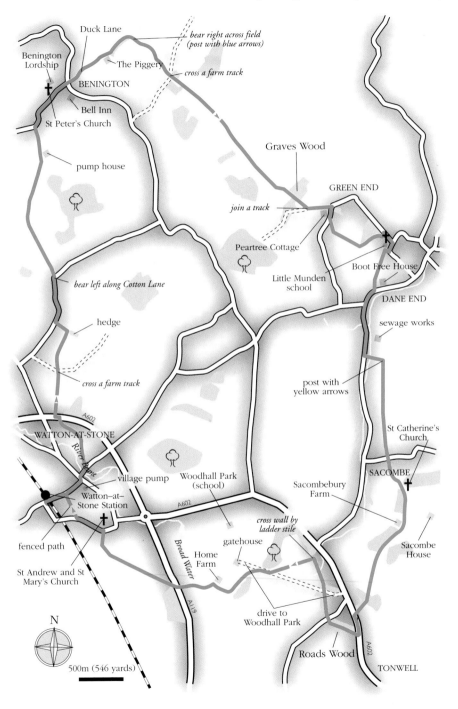

Duck Lane

bear right across field
(post with blue arrows)

Benington
Lordship

The Piggery

cross a farm track

BENINGTON

Graves Wood

Bell Inn
St Peter's Church

GREEN END

pump house

join a track

Peartree Cottage

Boot Free House

Little Munden
school

DANE END

bear left along Cotton Lane

hedge

sewage works

cross a farm track

post with
yellow arrows

St Catherine's
Church

WATTON-AT-STONE

River Beane

village pump

Woodhall Park
(school)

SACOMBE

Watton–at–
Stone Station

Sacombebury
Farm

fenced path

A602

cross wall by
ladder stile

Sacombe
House

St Andrew and St
Mary's Church

Broad Water

gatehouse

Home
Farm

drive to
Woodhall Park

A119

N

Roads Wood

A602

TONWELL

500m (546 yards)

Benington Lordship

Just along the road on the left are the iron gates that lead to Benington Lordship, a conglomeration of house and castle in a wonderfully eccentric mixture of architectural styles. The Lordship is based around the scanty ruin of a Norman stone keep built in 1138 by Roger de Valoignes without royal permission. The keep lasted fewer than 40 years; King Henry II had it destroyed, with the Royal Exchequer footing the bill for the hundred picks that were used to carry out the demolition. Various houses were erected on the moated site over the ensuing centuries; the present large red-brick structure was built around 1700, and the twin-towered folly of a gatehouse in 1832. Nowadays, Benington Lordship opens its beautiful gardens for a number of short display seasons every year: a summer rose garden, a sunken garden, autumnal shrubbery, a spectacular snowdrop display in late winter and other features.

Benington is centred on a medieval nucleus around the village green, with creaky old houses and cottages – many timber-framed – leaning this way and that. At the foot of Duck Lane there are ducks on the duck pond.

From the gates of Benington Lordship go forward to the T-junction (299237). For refreshment, turn right for the Bell Inn; to continue the walk keep ahead along Duck Lane ('PB Clay End 1¼, Green End 2½' fingerpost). Beside a house called The Piggery, keep ahead between two red-striped poles. In 400 yards (400m) you reach a post with blue arrows (306241), bear right here across a field. Soon a cross-hedge comes into view; aim for its left end. Keep forward here, at a post with blue arrows, aiming for the top right corner of the smaller of two woods ahead. Cross a farm track here (311237) and steer ahead along the bottom of the valley, keeping about 30 yards (30m) downhill of a line of trees. At the far end of the field join the valley bottom track (315234).

In 150 yards (150m) the track forks; keep right and continue through a hedge. At the gate at the far end of the next field keep ahead with a watercourse on your right and a hedge close on your left. At the end of this field go through a gate (322225 – blue arrow on a post), bear left, then in 10 yards (10m) bear right, following the field edge as it snakes and becomes a sunken lane rising to enter Graves Wood at the top left corner of the field (324224). In 300 yards (300m) join a track and keep forward to turn right along the road by Peartree Cottage (328223). In 40 yards (40m) leave the road and keep ahead ('Dane End ¾' fingerpost and 'No Horse Riding'

Opposite: The beautiful gardens of Benington Lordship, famous for their spring and summer displays, are kept in immaculate condition all year round.

notice). Follow the field edge with a hedge on your left. In 300 yards (300m) it bends left (329220 – yellow arrow); in another 300 yards (300m) continue ahead at two yellow arrows on a post with trees on your left. Soon the tower and stumpy spire of All Saints' Church at Little Munden (334219) heave into view. The path leads to a road where you turn right to pass the church and reach Little Munden school on the corner.

Turn right through the school gate and along the left-hand playground hedge for 20 yards (20m), then left through a gate and on across the field. Go through a kissing gate on the far side to cross a road; keep ahead along a path to cross another road, and ahead again (FP fingerpost) to the village road through Dane End (333214). Turn left here if you want to visit the Boot Free House; otherwise turn right along the road and out of Dane End. Cross a stream by a sewage works, and in 250 yards (250m) turn left (332207 – 'FP Potters Green 1, Whitehill 1' fingerpost) across a footbridge and up the field edge to a post with yellow arrows. Turn right with a bank on your left, which you follow for ¼ mile (1.2km) to a road (334196). Keep ahead up a rise, and turn left to pass St Catherine's Church, Sacombe (336194). Keep on along the track past a 'Private Road – Keep Out' sign (not applicable to walkers!) to pass Sacombebury Farm (336189) and continue along a drive through Sacombe Park for 1 mile (1.6km).

Sacombe Park

Here the character of the landscape changes. Up to now you have been walking through rolling Hertfordshire farming country, mostly arable, with field surfaces almost more flint than soil, and farmhouses sitting prominently on the clay ridges. Now the walk runs for 3 miles (5km) through the private parkland of Sacombe Park and Woodhall Park, with beautiful open grassland, feature trees, and an air of well-manicured orderliness.

Continue along the Sacombe Park drive to reach the A602 (331179). Cross the road (take care!) and turn left along the wide grass verge for 250 yards (250m), then turn right up steps and over a stile (331176 – FP fingerpost). Keep ahead along the field edge with a strip of woodland on your right, through the shank of Roads Wood and on to turn right along a road (327179). In 20 yards (20m) turn left ('FP Ware Road ½' fingerpost) down a field edge with a hedge on your left. Continue through a wood, crossing the long drive to Woodhall Park (327182). Leave the trees and follow the wall on your left to cross it by a ladder stile (326185). Keep forward by a yellow arrow on a pole to cross a stile and turn right along the Woodhall Park drive (321184), admiring the clock and cupola on the gatehouse of the mansion.

Woodhall Park

Woodhall Park (318185), now a school, was built around 1777 for Sir Thomas Rumbold, who had made his money serving the East India Company in whatever ways he could – probably none too scrupulously. He died in 1791, and the park was bought by another East India Company nabob, Paul Benfield, who had already been dismissed twice, suspended twice and investigated by the company. Eventually dismissed for good, Benfield was forced to take anything that came his way – it turned out to be a cool £0.5 million, a golden kiss-off from the East India Company. After retirement, Benfield speculated wildly in the city, and got himself elected MP for Shaftesbury – in those days a fabulously expensive operation. By 1805 he was broke, and had to sell Woodhall Park to meet his debts. He fled across the English Channel and died a lonely pauper in Paris in 1810.

In 150 yards (150m) bear left along the drive. Pass Home Farm, then turn left over a brick bridge to reach the A119 (314183). Cross the road (take care!) and go up the drive opposite, past the 'Strictly Private' notice. In 70 yards (70m) branch right off the drive (yellow arrow) and walk diagonally right across an open field. At the far side cross a stile (307184 – yellow arrow); continue through the trees, then on across the following field. At the far side cross a stile (303186) and bear right along a lane to meet the road in Watton Green.

Turn right along the road in Watton Green to St Andrew and St Mary's Church (302189), a fine flint-built church haunted by a Grey Lady who puts in an appearance twice a year. She threw herself off the church tower, local stories say, after being cruelly jilted. In front of the church bear left along the road ('Perrywood' sign). In 150 yards (150m) turn right (300190 – FP fingerpost) along a fenced path. Turn left at the top, then bear right to a road. Turn left to Watton-at-Stone Station.

BAYFORD, BRICKENDON, NEWGATE STREET & LITTLE BERKHAMSTED

Deep in the wooded farmlands of east Hertfordshire are ancient lanes used by travellers for hundreds of years, connecting farms and small settlements. Walking these lanes and the wood and field paths of the district you'll come across the all-but-forgotten five royal oaks on Brickendon Green, the fine country houses of Brickendon Grange, Ponsbourne Park, The Gage and Bayford House, as well as a preposterous and delightful tower called Stratton's Folly. There's also the classically pretty village of Little Berkhamsted, two of whose sons became celebrated in widely differing ways, and several beautiful stretches of woodland.

Start & Finish:	Bayford Station
Length of walk:	7 miles (11km)
OS maps:	1:50,000 Landranger 166; 1:25,000 Explorer 174, 182
Travel:	By rail from London King's Cross (35–45 mins); by road – M25 (Jct 25), A10 north to Hertford, B158 past County Hall, in 1½ miles (2.5km) left on minor road to Bayford and Brickendon.
Features:	Commemorative oaks on Brickendon Green; old hedges in the lane to Ponsbourne Park; Little Berkhamsted's pretty cottages; Stratton's Folly at Little Berkhamsted; Bayford Wood.
Refreshments:	Farmer's Boy PH, Brickendon; Coach and Horses PH, Newgate Street; Five Horseshoes PH, Little Berkhamsted; Baker Arms PH, Bayford.

Opposite: One of the many pleasures of walking in the Home Counties is the beautiful setting of handsome country houses and parks. Here, Ponsbourne Park sits neatly among pine and beech trees.

THE WALK

From Bayford Station (315083) walk up the station approach and turn left along the road. There's a nasty right-hand bend straight away, followed by ½ mile (0.75km) of steady climbing on a country road into Brickendon – but that gets the worst of the walk over right at the start!

Brickendon's memorial oaks

Like many Hertfordshire villages, Brickendon boasts a broad village green. The Farmer's Boy is a friendly local pub just along the road on the corner. Take a look at the little group of oak trees on the far side of the green (322079); they were planted over the span of a century to commemorate the coronations and jubilees of five British monarchs. The five inscribed memorial stones are still in place. Queen Victoria's oak has been reduced to a couple of stumps cut into the shape of rustic benches, and her stone has sunk so far into the turf that its inscription lies buried. The other stones read: 'ER VII 9 August 1902' (coronation of King Edward VII); a simple '1911' on a broken and uprooted stone (coronation of King George V); 'GR VI 1937' (coronation of King George VI); 'EIIR June 1977' (Silver Jubilee of Queen Elizabeth II). Poor love-wracked Edward VIII has neither oak nor stone, as he chose to abdicate before he could be crowned.

From the west side of Brickendon Green (320079) bear right along the side of the green ('White Stubbs Lane' FP fingerpost) to enter the grounds of Brickendon Grange Golf and Country Club. Pass the Grange (319077), now the golf club's clubhouse, a splendidly Gothic setting for some Hammer horror movie with its candlesnuffer turret and looming chimney stacks. The golfers are generally willing to show you the tortuous route through the golf course, which is marked with posts, mostly blue with one or two black.

Route through the golf course

Beyond Brickendon Grange, keep ahead past a pavilion on a gravel path. In 70 yards (70m) veer slightly right for a black post by an oak tree. Bear right to another blue post. Keep ahead past holly trees; in 50 yards (50m), at the end of a short row of conifers, bear left between a green and a bench. Keep on over the brow of the hill for 100 yards (100m), then bear right to a blue post. In 20 yards (20m) pass a hedge on your right, with a tall oak in the centre, to another blue post. Keep ahead on the same west-south-west line for 150 yards (150m) to a hedge. Bear left, following a line of blue posts in the hedge and a 'Safety Route' notice, along the edge of the wood to cross a stile and leave the golf course (315071).

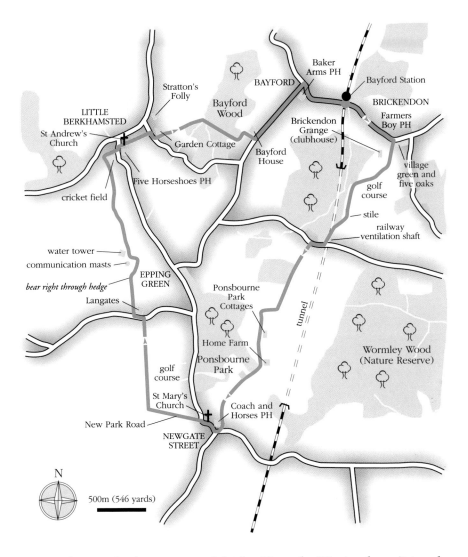

Keep the wood edge on your right for 20 yards (20m); where it trends away to the right, aim diagonally right ahead across the field to the angle of field, hedge and wood (313070). In the next field you'll pass a ventilation shaft for the 1½-mile (2.5-km) railway tunnel that runs directly below your boots here. The old Victorian brick cylinder of the shaft that rises from the grass has a fringe of weird-looking 'Ninja star'-style barbed wire and metal fortifications round its top to deter would-be shaft abseilers.

Lane to Ponsbourne Park

Cross a stile and turn right along the road, then in 70 yards (70m) turn left (312069) up a gravelled lane. This is a rough but beautiful 1½ miles (2.5km) of hedged country lane, with good views over arable farmland and across meadows where horses graze. Try the old rule-of-thumb method of dating the hedges; each separate species of bush or tree in a measured 100 yards (100m) stands for one century of age. The hedges you are walking between support oak, sycamore, lime, hawthorn, poplar, elder, blackthorn and horse chestnut – so they could be up to 800 years old.

After ½ mile (0.75km), follow the lane right and left through a dogleg; then you pass a run of model farmworkers' houses, Ponsbourne Park Cottages (307059), with a 1905 dragon emblem datestone. After passing the dilapidated buildings of Home Farm, walk down the drive of Ponsbourne Park (305056), a big pale-brick mansion peeping over trees, to turn right at the road (303050) past the Coach and Horses pub to the roundabout in the centre of Newgate Street village.

Keep ahead here for a few yards to pass St Mary's Church, where glorious angels uphold the octagonal spire on their outspread wings. Opposite the church, bear left down New Park Road for ⅓ mile (0.5km). Where the houses on the right peter out, turn right (295052 – FP fingerpost), aiming north with a hedge on your right along the edge of a golf course for ½ mile (0.75km) to a road (294061). Bear left for 100 yards (100m). Just past a house named Langates, turn right ('L. Berkhamsted 1½' FP fingerpost), crossing stiles and aiming for a cluster of communications masts and a water tower. In the third field, bear right through a metal kissing gate in the hedge (293065 – yellow arrow waymark); then follow up the right side of the hedge through two gates into a lane. Turn left past the masts and water tower; soon the leafy lane bends right, then continues ahead. In 300 yards (300m) it veers off to the right (292071); but keep ahead here in a tunnel of trees on a boggy bridleway. In ¼ mile (0.4km) go through a gate into fields. Keep ahead with a hedge on your right. Just before the road, bear right through a kissing gate (290077 – yellow-and-white waymark arrows), up the side of Little Berkhamsted's cricket field. At the road, facing the Five Horseshoes pub, turn left towards St Andrew's Church.

Little Berkhamsted

Little Berkhamsted could stand for the archetype of comfortable, neat little Hertfordshire villages. The lanes are lined with pretty cottages, many whitewashed and weatherboarded, in wonderfully cosseted gardens. St Andrew's Church stands under a charming stumpy broach spire. What a shame that it's kept locked, with no church porch notice of the whereabouts of the keyholder, so that few visitors make their way inside to admire the early 20th-century east window by the idiosyncratic artist-nobleman Rosencrantz. The village cricket field with its pile of sightscreens and well-seasoned pavilion seems ready for some classic match from a long-gone Golden Age. Very suitable, too, since Little Berkhamsted was the birthplace of one of cricket's truly great radio commentators, ever-lovable Brian Johnston, the immortal 'Jonners'.

Another honoured son of Little Berkhamsted was Thomas Ken, the 17th-century bishop of Bath and Wells, small of stature but huge of heart, who stood up to backsliding King Charles II like a hero and kept the common touch throughout his ministry. He gave away most of his money, and made a point of sitting down to dinner each Sunday in the company of the 12 poorest people he could find to invite. 'So lively and cheerful was his temper,' wrote Ken's biographer Sir John Hawkins, 'he would be very facetious and entertaining to his friends in the evening, even when it was perceived that with difficulty he kept his eyes open; and then seeming to go to rest with no other purpose than the refreshing and enabling him with more vigour and cheerfulness to sing his morning hymn, as he used to do to his lute before he put on his clothes.' What a sympathetic picture of the dark-complexioned little bishop that conjures up. Ken took enormous pleasure in playing, singing and composing: he wrote one of the best-loved hymns of all time, 'Awake, my soul, and with the sun'.

From the road, turn right just before the church (292078 – FP fingerpost) along the south side of the churchyard, and keep the hedge on your left through two fields to a road (295080).

Stratton's Folly

A tall tower rises beyond a wall 100 yards (100m) to your left. This splendid erection is Stratton's Folly, a great red-brick cylinder 100 feet (30m) high, in whose flanks you can see oriel, round and square windows climbing one above another to the crenellated cap of the tower. Colonel John Stratton built it in 1789, the better to view his ships in the River Thames, said locals, but it's more likely that he put up his great tower to aid his astronomical investigations.

Bayford Wood

Turn right along the road past Garden Cottage, then immediately left over a stile ('Bayford 1' FP fingerpost). To your right, the Elizabethan country house called The Gage lies low and pink-faced. Follow stiles and 'Hertfordshire Way' arrow waymarks for ½ mile (0.75km) to the footbridge into Bayford Wood (301081). Keep ahead up the woodland ride, following white arrow waymarks. Bayford Wood is a very fine example of a piece of coppice wood that has not been harvested for many years. The old beech coppice boles have 'shot' exuberantly, sending spindly limbs 50 feet (15m) into the air. The beeches here used to be highly specialised trees. Cutting them back to a low stump or 'stool' every few years produced a large number of long, slim side shoots which could be harvested for firewood or furniture-making. So the Bayford Wood trees were exploited until modern methods of husbandry did away with such old-fashioned practices.

Bayford Wood is quite beautiful to walk through at any time or season. Sounds are all muted: the trickle of a stream, the rustle of leaves underfoot, and bird song through the green filtered light under the beeches. The path climbs gently among the trees with white arrows painted on the tree trunks as waymarks. Near the top you cross a track; keep ahead here to leave Bayford Wood over a stile (303080). Keep the hedge on your left and follow it to the road. Across the hedge there are fine views of the great cedar trees and the mellow brick gables and tall chimneys of Bayford House. The old house's outbuildings make a harmonious ensemble, too, with the pepperpot turret of the stables rising among acres of tiled barn and shed roofs.

At the road (306079) turn left for the ½-mile (0.75-km) walk into Bayford village. Here you'll find the Baker Arms pub (311084), named in honour of Sir William Baker, alderman of the City of London, and builder of the grand Bayfordbury House just north of Bayford in the 1760s. Sir William had, in fact, been offered a baronetcy, with its automatic transferral of a knightly prefix to successive heirs; but he turned it down in favour of a simple knighthood with the dry comment that he would rather 'confine the folly to himself and entail no ridicule on his descendants'.

Just past the Baker Arms, bear right ('Bayford Station' sign) – please take great care on this sharp double bend! From here, it's a straight ⅓ mile (0.5km) to return to Bayford Station.

NEWPORT, WIDDINGTON & DEBDEN

The north-west corner of Essex is the most appealing part of the county, with a scatter of delightful medieval towns situated on roads and rivers that have brought prosperity via trade and travellers. The countryside is gently undulating clay land, with large flinty fields threaded by plenty of green lanes. Woods and hedges have not been grubbed out hereabouts, so the landscape wears a well-clothed look. Of the three settlements that you'll visit, Newport has several fine old houses and a parish church with a rare and beautiful painted chest; Widdington boasts its huge old Prior's Hall Barn; and Debden's church reveals a range of architectural styles, from ancient to modern. There are deer, owls, monkeys and flamingoes at Mole Hall Wildlife Park, and remnants of landscaped parkland around Debden.

Start & Finish:	Newport Station
Length of walk:	9 miles (14km)
OS maps:	1:50,000 Landranger 167; 1:25,000 Explorer 195
Travel:	By rail from London Liverpool Street (1 hr approx.); by road – M11 to Jct 9, B1383 to Newport.
Features:	Open country around Waldegraves Farm; Prior's Hall Barn, Widdington; Mole Hall Wildlife Park; Church of St Mary the Virgin and All Saints, Debden; St Mary's Church, Newport; Newport's main street.
Refreshments:	Fleur-de-Lys PH, Widdington; White Hart PH, Debden; White Horse Inn, Newport.

THE WALK

Cross the railway line at Newport Station (522336) and turn right along the lane; it climbs as a sunken lane up the left side of a great chalk pit (concrete PB fingerpost). At the top of the lane (529332) keep ahead with a hedge on your left through the fields for ½ mile (0.75km) to a road (536329). Bear left for 100 yards (100m); then at the left bend keep ahead ('Waldegraves Farm' sign) up a farm track, passing Waldegraves Farm and barns (538329). Waldegraves Farm is a nice old house, and the weatherboarded walls of its barns conceal much older frameworks of crooked, ancient timbers that were only roughly dressed by the carpenters before being erected. Follow the track across the middle of a field.

Around Waldegraves Farm

You'll get a 'roof-of-the-world' feeling as you walk through these big upland fields. This is open, airy country, well wooded and hedged, with sticky reddish clay in the fields. Map names tickle the fancy: Hanging Grove, Pig's Parlour, Cabbage Wood, London Jock Wood.

At the west corner of Cabbage Wood (544327) the bridleway continues ahead; but turn right here (concrete FP fingerpost and yellow arrow) across a field and down the right side of Park Wood. Cross a footbridge (543322) and follow the path across a field to the edge of a wood (541319). Turn right along the wood edge (yellow arrow). At the end of the wood, cross a small wooden footbridge, then walk directly across the field, ignoring – halfway – a post offering an alternative path to the left. Head for Widdington church, which you can see over to the right, walking past trees with houses behind them, until you arrive in the churchyard. Bear right round the church to reach the road at Widdington village green (538317). Turn right for ¼ mile (0.4km), then left (brown 'Prior's Hall Barn' sign) to reach Prior's Hall Barn (537317).

Prior's Hall Barn

This magnificent medieval barn forms part of a working farmyard. Other, lesser buildings stand nearby, so its full effect only hits home when you are standing inside this 'Cathedral of the Harvest', with its almost cathedral-like proportions: 124 feet (33m) long and 38 feet (11.5m) high. At one end stands the old raised threshing stage, its planking full of gaps. Gnarled oak timbers soar into the shadowy roof, to sprout side-shoots and curved supporting arms. Prior's Hall Barn is a north-west Essex aisled barn of crown post and collar purlin construction, say the architects. It was long thought to be of late 14th-century date; but dendrochronology (dating of its

Opposite: The carved base of the oriel window at Monk's Barn in Newport's main street shows the Coronation of the Blessed Virgin Mary. The Mother and Child are flanked by angels playing a harp and a pair of organs.

timbers) and the records of New College, Oxford, who originally ordered its construction on what was one of their Essex estates, have fixed it pretty firmly to 1440–42.

New College sold the barn to the Prior's Hall farmer in 1920. Up until 1976 it was still used for storing grain and straw, and must have been a splendid sight when full to the rafters. It had to be re-roofed during its restoration in 1977–83 using acres of red Sussex tiles. The original structure consumed 400 oaks, and it may not be too fanciful to say that there is something green and forest-like attached to this great barn's atmosphere.

From the barn, return to Widdington village green. The village sign, erected in honour of the recent millennium celebrations, shows Prior's Hall Barn, with one brown-habited monk scything corn and another gathering the stooks. Continue past the green and the Fleur-de-Lys pub; in 100 yards (100m) turn left along Cornells Lane ('Wildlife Park' sign). In ¼ mile (0.4km), at a double FP fingerpost, turn left through the hedge (541314), ignoring the first single fingerpost. Take the right-hand of the two paths, aiming diagonally right across a field for the right-hand corner of a wood on the far side, where you meet a road (547315).

Mole Hall Wildlife Park

If you want to visit the wildlife park (admission fee) turn right along the road to Cornells Lane; turn left here, then in 120 yards (120m) left again ('car park' sign) into the grounds of Mole Hall. This wildlife park displays beasts and birds in an agreeable jumble: fallow, sika and red deer; otters and wild cats; wallabies and llama-like guanacos; monkeys and lemurs; cranes and flamingoes. There are plenty of cuddly rabbits and guinea pigs, too. The house of Mole Hall is a wonderful early medieval hall on a moated site.

Back where the field path meets the road (547315), keep forward along the lane past Swayne's Hall entrance. Pass Mole Hall Farm, and continue along a green lane. In 40 yards (40m) a FP fingerpost points left; but keep straight ahead here on a green lane, which starts between hedges and then emerges to run along field edges (very muddy in wet conditions). After ½ mile (0.75km) it reaches a yellow arrow on a post, pointing right (554318). Ignore this, and keep ahead. In 300 yards (300m) the hedge turns right; keep ahead here, too. In 150 yards (150m) a blue 'bridleway' arrow on a post points ahead between hedges. After another 120 yards (120m) look for two blue arrows on a post on the right-hand side of the path (559319). Turn left here with a wood and then a hedge on your left. Soon you enter a green lane, which leads north to Rook End Lane (557325).

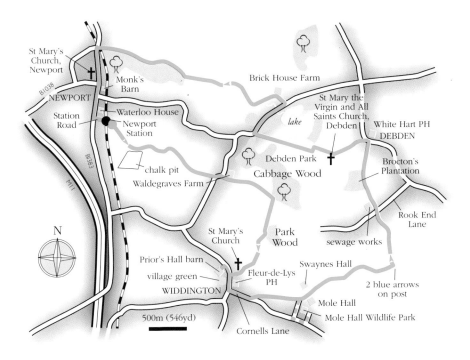

Cross Rook End Lane and head right to skirt a sewage works (FP fingerpost); then turn left up a field to walk along the right-hand side of Brocton's Plantation. At the end of the wood keep ahead with a hedge on your right to reach the road in Debden opposite the White Hart pub (556334). Turn left; in 50 yards (50m), on a sharp right bend, keep ahead ('Parish Church' sign) down a lane to reach Debden church (551332).

Church of St Mary the Virgin and All Saints, Debden
The 13th-century Church of St Mary the Virgin and All Saints is a curious mixture of architectural styles. The main body of the church has round Norman-looking pillars and gently pointed arches to the wide arcades. Up five steps there's a raised 18th-century chancel with an elaborate Moorish ceiling. At the north-east corner of the church a new late 20th-century brick extension, complete with pinnacles, has been tacked on. The west end of the church supports a stumpy weatherboarded bell turret topped with a fine Essex broach spire.

A stained-glass window inside the church displays the armorial devices of local families. A dove with an olive bough in its beak belongs to the Chiswells; a winged Star of David represents the Muilman clan; and the Trench family is signified by an upraised arm, its hand clutching a dagger. St Mary's is, frankly, a bit of a stylistic porridge, but one that is full of character. Its situation among dark yews in the bottom of a dell is striking, too, and lends the church a slightly sinister air.

You can either choose the path that crosses the churchyard or the one that runs round its perimeter. On the west side the path continues to join a vehicle track. Turn left at the track to cross an outlying limb of the great curved lake in Debden Park (549333). Keep ahead for 50 yards (50m); then turn right (FP sign) to cross two fields. Debden Hall, a handsome Georgian country house, was demolished in 1936; its extensive parkland still survives, centred on the lake. You can catch glimpses of this to your right as you move west through the fields.

At a road at the left corner of a wood (541335) turn right. Keep to the grass verge of the road for ¼ mile (0.5km). Cross a stream, then in 150 yards (150m) turn left through Brick House Farm gate (545338). Follow the left-hand of two FP fingerposts along a driveway below the farm. Pass a house, then, starting with the fence on your right, follow the valley bottom path (marked Bromley Lane on OS Explorer 195) for 1¼ miles (2.9km). Go under the railway (522345) to reach the B1383 in Newport, where you turn left along the main street. In ¼ mile (0.4km) cross the street and turn right up Wicken Road; walk up the sloping footpath and turn right along Church Street to St Mary's Church (521341).

St Mary's Church, Newport

Newport's church is a fine and elaborate flint structure with a great collection of strange gargoyles, more Eastern than European in inspiration: a lion, a monkey, a be-turbaned sage, a masked devil, and a Buddha-like figure with two cheeky little faces peeping out from the shelter of its jowls. The interior, tall and light, has some beautiful old stained glass in a pair of lancet windows in the west wall of the north transept. The top and bottom panels are a jumble of odd fragments, but each centre panel contains a coherent figure: St Katherine and her wheel of torture on the left and a partly armoured figure supporting a shield with a red cross – perhaps St George – on the right .

The chief treasure of the church, however, is the 13th-century altar chest in the south transept, its painted lid propped open as a reredos. A crucified Christ, his legs drawn up, is flanked by his mother and St John, their upper torsos drawn back in conventional but expressive attitudes of pain and horror, their mouths downturned. The artistry is direct but subtle, perfect in its simplicity.

The tomb of Robert Trappes (died 1526) carries brasses of this well-to-do Tudor merchant and his two wives. They look a sleek and prosperous trio, but their epitaph soberly points out the vanity and brevity of worldly goods and fame:

> When the bells be merrely roung
> And the masse devoutly soung
> And the meate merrely eaten
> Then shall Robert Trappes, his wiffs and children be forgotten.

Newport

Back on the main street, turn right and continue to walk along. On the left you'll find the 15th-century Monk's Barn, with many oak studs filled in with herringbone-pattern brickwork. One projecting window has a carved beam, rather eroded by weather, on which you can make out a religious scene: the Coronation of the Virgin Mary. She sits grasping a sceptre with a curly-haired Jesus on her left hand, while angels hymn her from both sides with a pipe organ and a harp.

There are handsome brick Georgian buildings along the street, and striking over-sailing black-and-white gables in the Old Vicarage. Above the shop window of Waterloo House sits a bust of a Civil War personage with curly moustaches and an armoured collar and throat guard. It could be Oliver Cromwell, but is more likely to represent King Charles I. The king was at Newport when Sir Harbottle Grimston of Colchester made a dramatic petition, kneeling while he pleaded for Charles to come to a peaceful accommodation with Parliament and prevent yet more bloodshed. But the king refused to listen, preferring to continue down the path that eventually led to his own execution in 1649.

At the foot of the town, turn left along Station Road to reach Newport Station.

KELVEDON, COGGESHALL & FEERING

From Kelvedon you walk out through gentle Essex farming countryside, passing tranquil Pointwell Mill to stroll beside the River Blackwater up to Coggeshall Abbey. In the beautiful little town of Coggeshall there is a wealth of medieval building to admire – notably the ancient Grange Barn, and the richly carved wool-merchant's house of Paycocke's – before setting back south across the fields. All Saints at Feering is a wonderful church, with a replica John Constable altarpiece as one of its treasures. And don't forget to leave enough time, before catching your train, to explore the handsome houses along Kelvedon's long main street.

Start & Finish:	Kelvedon Station
Length of walk:	7½ miles (12.5km)
OS maps:	1:50,000 Landranger 168, 1:25,000 Explorers 183, 195
Travel:	By rail from London Liverpool Street (50 mins); by road – M25 (Jct 28), A12.
Features:	Pointwell Mill; Coggeshall Abbey buildings; Grange Barn; Paycocke's, Church of St Peter-ad-Vincula, Woolpack Inn and many buildings at Coggeshall; All Saints' Church, Feering.
Refreshments:	Woolpack Inn, Coggeshall; Bell Inn, Feering.

THE WALK

Kelvedon is a pleasant little town straggling out along what was the main road from Colchester to London before the A12 bypass was built. Looking

Opposite: A beautiful modern terracotta bas-relief of the Virgin and Child fills the niche over the south porch doorway at All Saints' Church, Feering. Designed by Stella King, the bas-relief was baked at the local specialist brickworks in Bulmer.

down the straight line of the street, it's no surprise to learn that this was a Roman road. The Romans knew Kelvedon as Canonium. They built their town on the site of a Belgic village, with the River Blackwater guaranteeing a constant supply of water. The river wriggles under a bridge not far from the railway station, and cradles the south part of the town. The High Street is lined with 18th-century houses, and plenty of much older ones too, all very easy on the eye.

If you want to explore Kelvedon's High Street straight away, turn right out of the station car-park (863193). To start the walk, however, turn left from the station along the road. At the first left bend, turn right through a gate (863195 – FP fingerpost) and keep ahead along the field edge with a willow grove and the River Blackwater on your right. At the end of the first field, aim diagonally left across the next field to go through a gap in the hedge (this field may be ploughed/sown). Follow a line the width of a tractor that bisects the field – it may be an old field boundary or the remains of a green lane – keeping ahead to the skyline (862203). Here you join a lane for ¹/₂ mile (0.75km), passing Coggeshall Hall to reach a row of poplars (858210 – yellow arrows on a post). Aim diagonally left across the next field (also ploughed/sown), passing to the right of a big depression to reach the road 200 yards (200m) to the right of a line of cottages (855211 – concrete FP fingerpost). Turn right for an unpleasant but inescapable ¹/₄ mile (0.4km) of road, with a grass verge most of the way, into Coggeshall Hamlet. Just past the telephone box, turn right down Pointwell Lane to reach Pointwell Mill (853215).

Pointwell Mill

This is a delightful picture: the old brick-built mill and a bent weatherboarded cottage side by side, fronted by weeping willows and undercut by a sluicing millstream. The cottage could be up to 700 years old, thinks the mill owner – that would make it nearly contemporary with Pointwell's sister mill at Coggeshall Abbey, ¹/₂ mile (0.75km) up the River Blackwater.

To reach the abbey mill and buildings on the outskirts of Coggeshall, walk round Pointwell Mill house (yellow arrows on a gatepost and shed wall), over a bridge and through an iron gate to continue forward along the right bank of the mill stream. Near Coggeshall Abbey the stream divides (855220); cross a bridge to follow the right-hand channel until you are opposite the abbey buildings, then turn left over the mill bridge (855222) and through the farmyard beside the ancient Chapel of St Nicholas.

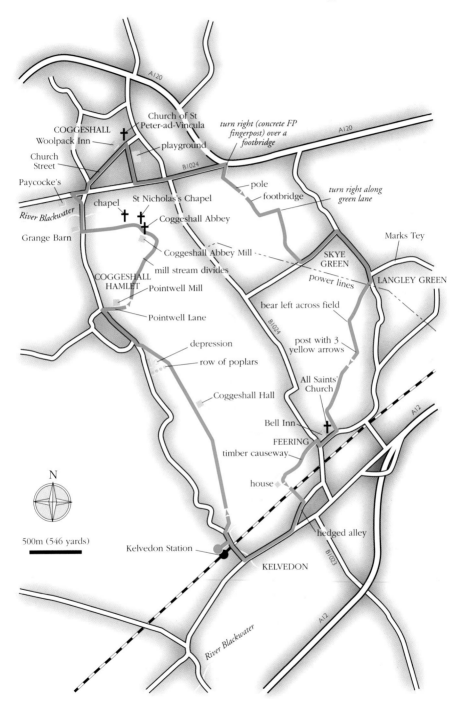

Church of St
Peter-ad-Vincula

COGGESHALL
Woolpack Inn

*turn right (concrete FP
fingerpost) over a
footbridge*

playground

Church
Street

B1024

Paycocke's

pole

*turn right along
green lane*

footbridge

River Blackwater

chapel   St Nicholas's Chapel

Marks Tey

Coggeshall Abbey

Grange Barn

Coggeshall Abbey Mill

SKYE
GREEN

mill stream divides

power lines

LANGLEY GREEN

COGGESHALL
HAMLET

Pointwell Mill

bear left across field

B1024

Pointwell Lane

depression

post with 3
yellow arrows

row of poplars

All Saints'
Church

Coggeshall Hall

Bell Inn

N

FEERING

timber causeway

house

A12

500m (546 yards)

hedged alley

Kelvedon Station

B1023

KELVEDON

A12

River Blackwater

Coggeshall Abbey

Coggeshall Abbey is one of those secluded English spots that stays in the mind as an epitome of peace and time-suspended beauty. On one hand you have the old weatherboarded mill, bowed under its big sloping tiled roofs and tall chimney, half drowned in greenery. On the other stands the handsome pink-washed Elizabethan house that was built on the foundations of Coggeshall Abbey some 50 years after the monastery was shut and destroyed on the orders of King Henry VIII. Protectively surrounding the house are outbuildings and ancillary quarters where you can trace the outlines of cloister arches, doorways, lancet windows and sections of wall from the Cistercian abbey that was founded in the 1140s.

The red-brick Chapel of St Nicholas, with its four brick-framed lancet windows, is a rarity; it was built as the gate chapel of Coggeshall Abbey around 1225, an extraordinarily early date to be using newly made brick. The art of brick and tile making lapsed in Britain for some 800 years after the Romans left around AD 410. Almost all brick building predating the 14th century re-uses Roman materials, so to see building with thicker bricks than the Romans ever employed, evidently made specifically for the construction of this handsome little chapel, is to witness a moment of architectural history established and then frozen in time.

In front of the abbey buildings stand cattle sheds and stables. Cows and horses, hens and ducks, hay bales and fruit orchards – Coggeshall Abbey still has an aura of rural self-sufficiency. From the abbey, walk up the drive, passing another chapel (Essex Way/EW marker stone nearby) to reach the road (850222). Turn right to find Grange Barn on your left (848222).

Coggeshall Grange Barn

The Grange Barn at Coggeshall is one of Europe's oldest barns – probably the oldest, in fact. This mighty 'Cathedral of the Harvest' is estimated to date back to around 1140, about the same time as the foundation of Coggeshall Abbey. By the late 20th century it was a gap-roofed ruin, far too big for modern farming needs, far too expensive and difficult for one farmer to keep in repair in an era when the number of men employed around the farm had plummeted. But the Coggeshall Grange Barn Trust was formed by local enthusiasts, and with help from the district and county councils they put it back into tiptop order during the 1980s. It is a highly atmospheric building, with a bare dry forest of timbers rising and spreading to hold up the enormous area of tiles that make up the great barn roof.

From Grange Barn continue down the road to cross the River Blackwater. Further down the road, cross a stream by an iron bridge and bear left, then left again along Coggeshall's main street ('Braintree' sign) to find Paycocke's 100 yards (100m) along on the left (848225).

Paycocke's

Paycocke's was built around 1505 by Coggeshall woolman John Paycocke for his clothier son Thomas. It is a magnificent specimen of a nouveau-riche Tudor woolmaster's house, an outward and visible measurement of the householder's wealth in richness of woodcarving and acreage of timber and glass. The silvery wood of the façade timbers is heavily carved. Among the embellishments are a grinning figure bearing a shield embossed with a leering face, a king and queen intimately entwined, a beggar and a priest, a jester in a pointed cap and an upside-down dragon – all these enmeshed in foliage. There are tall flanking figures to the big carriage doorway and many other enjoyable details to be spotted. Inside the house is a high-ceilinged hall with beautifully carved oak timbers, a dining room with rich linenfold panelling and a fireplace carved with lions, deer and dogs, and a little sitting room where exquisite 19th-century Coggeshall lace is displayed. Upstairs there is more linenfold panelling and ceiling-beam embellishment in the two bedrooms and a fireplace surround carved with a bristle-backed boar, a unicorn and a strange diplodocus-like beast.

Leaving Paycocke's, turn right to return up the street. Opposite the White Hart Hotel turn left, then immediately right along Church Street ('Earl's Colne' sign) for ½ mile (0.75km) to pass the 15th-century Woolpack Inn – beamed, gabled, with crooked walls and charm to burn – and reach the Church of St Peter-ad-Vincula (854230).

Church of St Peter-ad-Vincula, Coggeshall

St Peter's Church was built around the same time as the Woolpack Inn, and beautified by the rich woolmen of Coggeshall. You'll find brasses to the Paycockes in the floor of the north chapel, and on the south chapel wall there is a memorial to the remarkably fecund and long-lived Margaret Honywood. At her death in 1620 she left 367 descendants – 16 children, 164 grandchildren, 228 great-grandchildren and nine great-great-grandchildren.

From the church, cross the road. Bear left for 30 yards (30m), then right down a path (EW fingerpost) past a playground. Continue across a playing field to the B1024 (855226). Turn left and walk on the pavement for ½ mile (0.75km) (ignoring an EW fingerpost on the right), until the road bends left to join the A120. Keep ahead here (862228) along a cul-de-sac road for 100 yards (100m), then turn right (fallen concrete FP fingerpost) over a wooden footbridge. Continue along the field edge for 100 yards (100m).

Just past a telephone pole turn left through the hedge (yellow arrow on a post). In the field beyond (again ploughed/sown), aim ahead for the pole in the middle of the field (a pylon is seen beyond and a little to the right), then make for the innermost part of the curve in the far hedge to cross a grassy bank over a ditch (865225). Aim slightly right to a post on the far side of the next field. Turn left (yellow arrow) to walk along the field edge. In 150 yards (150m) the hedge on your right comes to an end, but keep ahead across the shank of the field for 50 yards (50m) to turn right along a green lane, following the Essex Way.

At the end of the lane (870219) turn left along the road, then right at a T-junction ('Feering, Kelvedon' sign). Continue to Langley Green where the Marks Tey road turns left, bear right here (876218 – FP fingerpost) along a field edge with a hedge on your left and under power lines. At the end of the field turn left over a footbridge, then bear right (yellow arrows) with the hedge on your right. In 130 yards (130m) bear diagonally left (874214) across the field, aiming for the left end of the hedge on the far side (post with three yellow arrows). Turn right along the field edge, with the hedge on your right, to go through the corner of the next hedge. Bear diagonally left here (873209 – yellow arrow on post) on a clear path towards Feering church. At the far corner of the field go through the hedge, and continue towards the church with a hedge on your left. At the next field corner, bear left (872206 – yellow arrow on post) to a road and turn right to Feering church (872204).

All Saints' Church, Feering

All Saints' Church has a fine tall Tudor brick porch; its niche holds a modern terracotta bas-relief of the Virgin and Child. Inside you'll find some fascinating old glass in a north window and two alabaster statues from Colne Priory dated to around 1400 – that of the Virgin and Child supported by little censing angels is especially beautiful. In the north or Lady Chapel hangs a *Risen Christ* altarpiece, a replica of that painted by John Constable in 1822. The original, which once graced the church, is now retained by the Constable Trust in nearby Dedham. Christ leans back with his arms wide and hands outstretched, a white cloak billowing around him and a fiery sky as a background – a most dramatic depiction.

From the church, pass the Bell Inn to reach the B1024. Turn right, then in 10 yards (10m) turn left through a wicket gate (concrete FP fingerpost and 'No cycling' symbol) along a path. It crosses a bog by a timber causeway, then continues as a grassy path. At a house the path bends left alongside a cricket ground (868200) to run under the railway. In 150 yards (150m) turn right along a hedged alley (870198 – FP fingerpost). At the road (869195) turn right into Kelvedon to return to the station.

INGATESTONE, BUTTSBURY & MOUNTNESSING HALL

In the gently rolling farming landscape north-east of Brentwood sits Ingatestone Hall, a superb Tudor mansion built by a poor man's son who made good: he became Privy Councillor to four of the five great Tudor monarchs. The hall forms the centrepiece of this walk, which also takes in a pretty chapel on a ridge, stables and horse paddocks down in the valley of the River Wid, and the handsome house-and-church grouping at Mountnessing Hall.

Start & Finish:	Ingatestone
Length of walk:	7 miles (11km)
OS maps:	1:50,000 Landranger 167 or 177; 1:25,000 Explorer 175
Travel:	By rail from London Liverpool Street (35–40 mins); by road – M25 (Jct 28), A12 to Ingatestone.
Features:	Church of St Edmund and St Mary, Ingatestone; Ingatestone Hall; Buttsbury Chapel; horse paddocks and stables between Buckwyns Farm and Hannikin's Farm; Mountnessing Hall and Church of St Giles Mountnessing; Westlands Farm and Tilehurst.
Refreshments:	Plenty of pubs and refreshments in Ingatestone.

THE WALK

The architecture of Ingatestone Station (650992) is a fine example of the sensitivity with which the early railway companies had to tread. The Eastern Counties Railway Company must have been well aware, when they were planning their new line from London to Colchester in the 1830s, that Lord Petre of Ingatestone Hall, a powerful and canny figure who needed to be placated, owned a fine Elizabethan country house that stood less than a mile from the proposed route of the railway. So the station they provided for Ingatestone when the line opened in 1841 is a brave – and fairly successful – stab at mock-Elizabethan, a red-brick building with diamond patterns inset in dark brick, lattice windows and tall mock-Tudor chimneys. It makes a grand gateway to this walk.

Leaving the station building, turn right along the fenced path beside the station car-park ('No bicycles' notice). Soon the path reaches the village playing field – known as Fair Field – and runs up the left-hand side to reach the Church of St Edmund and St Mary (651996).

Church of St Edmund and St Mary, Ingatestone

The children of Ingatestone play on swings and slides in the shadow of the tremendous church tower. Four storeys high, sporting a set of battlements and recessed Romanesque window frames, this is a remarkable essay in red-brick construction. The church itself is a hotchpotch of component materials: bricks, tiles, flint cobbles, ragstone chunks and quartzite pebbles. Sadly, this gorgeous building is kept locked, but if you are lucky enough to find the church open, or plan ahead by contacting the church wardens, you'll enjoy some notable Elizabethan and Jacobean tombs of the Petre family of Ingatestone Hall – especially that of Sir William Petre (died 1572), founder of the family's fortunes. He was the son of a tanner from Devonshire and worked his way up, as a bright young Elizabethan lawyer could do in that Golden Age of self-confidence and open opportunities. William eventually served as Secretary of State to King Henry VIII, and was Privy Councillor to no fewer than four Tudor monarchs: Henry and his three offspring, King Edward VI, Queen Mary and Queen Elizabeth I.

To reach the splendid country house built by Sir William Petre, return from the church across Fair Field, aiming between the pond and the cricket pavilion to reach a grassy path that crosses the railway line (652994). Follow the path across the field and under power lines, aiming for Ingatestone Hall Farm. At the far side of the field, cross a stile and keep ahead with a fence on your left. Just before the farm, yellow arrows on a fence post (653987) give you a choice: left to continue the walk, or right to the gates of Ingatestone Hall.

Ingatestone Hall

Ingatestone Hall (654985) is a really fine Tudor country house, exactly the kind of rambling, extensive domain you would expect a Privy Councillor to possess. William Petre certainly knew how to seize his chances when they

Opposite: *Buttsbury Chapel, with its stumpy weatherboarded bell-tower, is a fine example of the remote country churches perched on clay ridges that are a common feature of the rural Essex landscape.*

came. In 1535 he was assistant to Thomas Cromwell when King Henry VIII's Chief Secretary was weighing up the wealth of the monasteries prior to their dissolution. Cromwell sent Petre to Essex to list the monasteries' holdings there, and when the young lawyer saw Barking Abbey's manor of Yenge-atte-Stone (Ingatestone) he coveted it on sight and took out a lease on it. The handsome house he built on the site in the 1540s had piped water and flush-through drains, so it was modern and comfortable as well as impressive. Ingatestone Hall has reduced in size over the centuries, but still remains eye-catching with its ranks of mullioned and latticed windows, acres of tiled roofs, crowstepped gables and castellated turrets.

You approach the house through a fine half-timbered gatehouse surmounted by a clock tower. The clock has only one hand, but keeps the hours efficiently as it has done for 250 years. The Petre family motto, 'Sans Dieu Rien' – 'Without God, Nothing' – appears under the clock, a suitably pious tag for a family that maintained its Catholic faith throughout the worst phases of persecution in Tudor and Stuart times. Inside the house you can see the cramped, claustrophobic hidey-holes – one in the study, the other in a concealed chamber off the staircase – where evidence of the Petres' illegal adherence to their faith could be hidden if the authorities were about. Catholic priests may have been concealed, but the holes were probably for Mass vestments and plate. Priests were certainly welcomed at Ingatestone Hall; they pretended to be members of the household, though a wagging tongue could betray them at any time, as happened to the Jesuit priest John Payne, who was arrested after a fellow servant gave him away. The punishment meted out to Payne – he was hanged, drawn and quartered in public in the market square at Chelmsford in 1582 – hung over the heads of all these brave men, smuggled into England from exile and hidden in great recusant houses like Ingatestone.

Other interesting features of the interior of the hall are the drawing room with its forest of deer antlers on the walls and its rare George Stubbs portraits of the 9th and the 10th Lord Petre; the dining room with fine linenfold oaken panelling and a splendidly vigorous tapestry depicting St George efficiently despatching the dragon with sword and lance; and the 95 feet- (29m-) long gallery hung with portraits of the family, including a wise and rather cagey-looking Sir William, builder of the house. Anyone who managed to retain his Catholic faith, and his head, while serving four monarchs with opinions as divergent and fiercely held as those of the Tudors, must have been exceptionally crafty.

From Ingatestone Hall return to the post with yellow arrows just above the farm (653987). Walk ahead along the side of the hall grounds, with good views of its roofs, turrets and chimneys. Follow yellow arrow

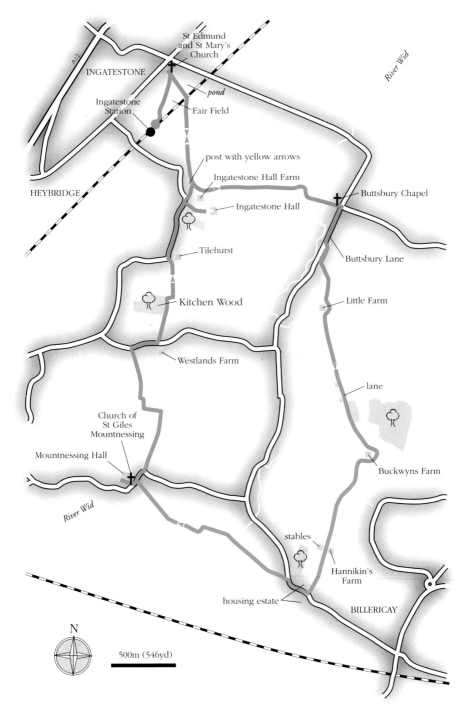

waymarks through the Essex farming countryside of wide fields with spreading hedge oaks and rocket-shaped poplars. Cross the left-hand footbridge over the River Wid (661987) and follow the river bank to the right; then aim ahead to Buttsbury Chapel on the ridge (664986).

Buttsbury Chapel

This 14th-century chapel, sheltered among its trees, has the beauty of simplicity. Its weatherboarded bell turret is crowned by a ball finial. The north door has enormous elaborate curly iron hinges. Graffiti of the 18th and 19th centuries is incised around the doorway in the weatherboarded south porch. Inside, a wall tablet pays a movingly direct tribute to Edward Freeman Hudson (1906–89), '50 years a Clerk in Holy Orders, Vicar of the Parish from 1952 to 1988: A loving Priest and true friend to all'.

From the chapel bear right down Buttsbury Lane. Pass a house on the left, and at the next field hedge on the left cross a footbridge and stile (662982). Aim diagonally across the field to cross another footbridge and follow the path along the hedge and through Little Farm. Continue with a fence on your right to meet the River Wid in the valley bottom (663976). Cross a small tributary that flows into the river here and follow the river (keeping it on your right) up to a fence. Turn left at the fence and cross a stile in the hedge (yellow arrow) into a shady lane. At the end of the lane, cross a road and go over a stile (664970 – 'Public footpath 183 to Buckwyns' fingerpost), passing through scrubby trees to cross a fence (yellow arrow) and keep ahead up a lane and then the drive of Buckwyns Farm (666968). Just before the house, the path swings left (yellow arrow) to make three sides of a square round the house. On the far side (665967 – south-west corner), yellow arrows direct you south to cross a stream by a footbridge, cross two fields and then walk south-south-west for ½ mile (0.75km), between a paddock fence and a hedge, and through Hannikin's Farm stable yard (663961).

Horse country

The lanes that thread this lush, dampish valley bottom are overhung with hazel and lime trees. There are tangled old orchards, and patches overgrown with stubby oaks like damp commons. The green meadows have been fenced off to make paddocks, and in the fields between Buckwyns Farm and Hannikin's Farm (two fine medieval yeomen's names) you'll see plenty of horses grazing. There's a wild, slightly anarchic feel to these rather ramshackle farms and small horse businesses, in contrast to the neat, house-proud estates of north Billericay into whose outskirts you now walk.

At the end of the lane (662958) keep ahead through the housing estate. In 100 yards (100m) you reach a T-junction and turn right along the road.

In 150 yards (150m), at a right-hand bend, go left (660958 – 'Footpath 199' fingerpost) and keep forward between the field edge and a fence. After three fields, turn left on reaching the River Wid and cross it on the first footbridge you reach (656961). Aim ahead to the left of a house. Cross a stile over a fence; continue, then cross a stile into a lane (653962). Turn left; in 10 yards (10m) go right through the hedge and over a footbridge. Keep ahead across the fields, aiming just to the left of Mountnessing's church spire. Cross a stile and the road to reach the church (648966).

Church of St Giles Mountnessing and Mountnessing Hall
The Church of St Giles Mountnessing makes a compact huddle – a low brick chancel, a taller flint nave butted up close, and a weatherboarded tower with a shingled broach spire riding high on a wide brick west-end gable. Like so many Essex churches, St Giles's is kept locked, so you will be lucky to make your way inside and see the six timber posts and the braces holding up the free-standing belfry, the chancel's reredos of Moses and Aaron, and the great 13th-century parish chest cut from a single log.

Just beyond the church stands Mountnessing Hall, a beautiful building with a seven-bay façade of weather-darkened Georgian brick, tall chimneys and a pretty walled garden. St Giles's stands at its shoulder, the two buildings making a harmonious pairing like a long-married couple.

At St Giles's, follow the path (concrete 'FP' fingerpost) through the churchyard to its north-east corner, go through the hedge and bear left (649967) along the field-edge path with a hedge on your right. At the far end of the field, follow the field edge round to the left (blue and yellow arrows). In 130 yards (130m) turn right through the hedge (649971 – blue and yellow arrows), following a path in a woodland shelter strip. Leave the trees and keep ahead across a field to a road by a house (648975). Turn right for 200 yards (200m). Opposite Westlands Farm turn left (concrete 'FP' fingerpost) up the right side of Kitchen Wood. At the top of the wood dogleg right, then left (651979), and keep ahead to reach Tilehurst.

Westlands Farm (650975) and Tilehurst (652982) are two fine examples of their type. Westlands is a dignified, square Georgian brick house, with an ancient barn-cum-house beside it. The older building has a bulging, black-timbered end, and is topped by a weathervane fox. The fox has lost his brush – to some local sharpshooter, judging by the number of bullet holes in his body. Tilehurst is a great pile of a country house with many half-timbered gables in a vast acreage of brick under a lead-domed turret: a Gothic murder mansion behind its walls and railings.

Arriving opposite Tilehurst, bear left to reach the road. Turn right to reach Ingatestone Hall, from where you retrace your steps to the railway station.

ROCHFORD & PAGLESHAM

This fine long walk takes you way out into the wilds of easternmost Essex, a country divided between flat arable farmlands and muddy creeks. Wildfowl throng here, so the bird-watching is tremendous. You'll encounter stories of an 18th-century adventurer, and of a smuggler chief who munched wineglasses and wrestled a bull. Paglesham Churchend is one of Essex's most charming villages. Above all, the walk – the loneliest in this book – is steeped in the salty sights and sounds of the broad, tidal River Roach.

Start & Finish: Rochford Station
Length of walk: 14 miles (22km)
OS maps: 1:50,000 Landranger 178; 1:25,000 Explorer 176
Travel: By rail from London Liverpool Street (50 mins); by road – M25 (Jct 29), A127 to northern outskirts of Southend-on-Sea, B1013 to Rochford.
Features: Rochford Hall; St Andrew's Church, Rochford; River Roach and its bird life (don't forget your binoculars and bird book!); Paglesham's two fine pubs; church and village street at Paglesham Churchend.
Refreshments: Plough and Sail PH, Paglesham Eastend; Punch Bowl PH, Paglesham Churchend; Cherry Tree PH (890908) on eastern outskirts of Rochford.

THE WALK

At Rochford Station (873904), cross the railway line using the footbridge and take the zigzagging tarmac path out of the station. At the bottom of the path turn left onto a tarmac lane; soon, the surface underfoot becomes concrete. As you walk along you will notice to your right Rochford Hall (870903), in the near distance, and St Andrew's Church.

Rochford Hall and St Andrew's Church
'Rochford Hall,' says Rochford Hundred Historical Society's blue plaque by the front door of the house, 'Home of the Boleyn family, 1515 to 1542'.

A strange attribution, since this fine Tudor house with its four gables and octagonal corner turret was probably built around 1545. Whatever the house that stood on the site then, it is claimed to be the birthplace of Anne Boleyn around 1504. Her father, Sir Thomas Boleyn, was created Viscount Rochford in 1525 by King Henry VIII, who was to involve himself closely, and disastrously, with this Essex family (see pages 126–32). Poor, doomed Anne, with her passionate red hair and her rumoured 'devil's teat' sixth finger, seemed destined for a strange fate. Failing to present her husband the king with a son and heir, she was beheaded at the Tower of London in 1536 by a French swordsman specially shipped over to London for the occasion.

The adjacent St Andrew's Church boasts a tall three-storey brick tower. The church walls are a characterful mishmash of clunch blocks, ragstone and flint, with crude chequered battlements of flushwork (knapped flint and freestone) to the south porch and south aisle. The north side of the church, with its two half-timbered gables and tall brick chimneys, looks remarkably like a medieval house.

Walk past the hall and church. The lane ends on a golf course. Keep ahead with a hedge on your left. At the hedge end continue, to cross a bridge (873901 – yellow arrow), and keep ahead for 50 yards (50m) to a post with a yellow arrow pointing left. Follow the arrow across the golf course fairways (beware the ball that flieth by day!) to reach a white wicket gate and cross the railway (875900). This crossing is on the level – so please stop, look and listen! Keep ahead along the cul-de-sac to cross a busy road (877900 – concrete PB fingerpost and yellow arrow) and keep ahead along Tinkers Lane. In 300 yards (300m) a yellow arrow on an iron post points forward, but turn left here along a tree-tunnel path for 200 yards (200m). At the end (879902) turn right along the Roach Valley Way (RVW), with the River Roach on your left. In ½ mile (0.75km), at the imposing Stambridge Mills, cross the mudflats on a footbridge and follow the path round the buildings. At the road turn left (887904 – RVW symbol and yellow arrow); in 70 yards (70m) go right (RVW and concrete FP fingerpost) across a field and a reed pond (private fishery) by a footbridge.

The Roach Valley Way symbol is a Canada goose flying over a reedbed on a broad river, with a church tower peeping among trees in the background. It sums up perfectly the character of the River Roach landscape. The river itself, inland of its estuary, is a winding, muddy stream fringed with reeds and sedges and overhung with alder and poplar trees, a moody watercourse in tune with its flat, lowland landscape.

From the footbridge keep ahead through trees to cross a cricket field. At the road (891904) bear right through a wooden gate and along a green lane

(RVW); at the bottom turn left along the River Roach (now on your right) on a seawall path that runs for 5½ miles (9km) to Paglesham Eastend. The only deviation necessary is at Barton Hall (913913), where the seawall disappears: walk ¼ mile (0.4km) across the marsh to rejoin the seawall just beyond the farm.

An ardent adventurer

Where you join the river bank, spare a look back towards Stambridge Mills and the scatter of rusty trawlers among the yachts and dinghies in the marina. Between you and the mill stands the river-bank house of Broomhills (888903). In the late 18th century it was the home of John Harriott, a most remarkable adventurer. Born in the parish of Great Stambridge in 1745, this ardent youth catapulted himself into a rackety, exciting life after reading *Robinson Crusoe*. He started off by voyaging to New York as a midshipman in a Royal Navy warship. Soon he had embroiled himself in a romantic mystery involving rescuing an Irish woman from captivity and returning her to her family.

After cruising in the Mediterranean, Harriott had to be saved when his ship was wrecked. Nothing daunted, he volunteered for sea duty again, and was present at the attack on Havana, Cuba. After that he travelled east by sea to St Petersburg, then west again to Jamaica where he fought and survived a duel. By 1766 he was back in America, a sworn member of a Native American tribe. The settled life didn't hold Harriott, however: he was still no more than 21 years old, still full of pith and vinegar. Off he went to India, to join the East India Company's campaign against Hyder Ali. During the fighting he was wounded and shipped back home.

That put paid to the Essex Man's foreign jaunting. He took up the life of a farmer, along with dabbling in insurance broking. Harriott remained hot to handle, however. He lost all his money investing unwisely in the spirit trade. Sited as he was, here on the banks of a river notorious in that era for smuggling, he must have dabbled in the contraband 'free trade', too. But Harriott had his conscientious side as well (unless it was a clever blind), for he organised the first force of river police to patrol the Thames. All in all, a true 18th-century maverick.

Wildfowl paradise of the Roach muds and marshes

Walking east along the seawall of the River Roach, two impressions strike

Opposite: Rochford Hall, where the beautiful but doomed Anne Boleyn is reputed to have been born c. 1504. Her passionate love affair and short, stormy marriage to Henry VIII led to the ruination of the ambitious Boleyn family.

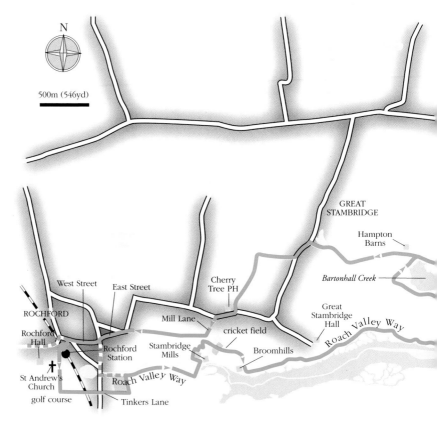

home immediately: the extreme flatness of the landscape, and the tremendous abundance of birdlife. This eastern part of Essex lies very flat, and views across the fields run a long way. Willows, hedge oaks, pylons and the block-like shapes of houses and barns loom up against the sky as if magnified to twice the size. The rivers wind towards their North Sea mouths through fringes of saltmarsh held together with thick tangled mats of sea purslane and seamed with sinuous tidal creeks. The Roach has built up vast mud banks, each square yard of mud packed with invertebrate and crustacean life. These flats make superb natural larders for waders, ducks and geese. In late autumn, millions of birds arrive from the Arctic Circle to spend the winter on the Essex estuaries, and the Roach gets its fair share. But these muds and marshes attract birds all the year round. Binoculars will enhance your enjoyment of the feeding, courting and squabbling of ringed plover, terns, redshank and curlew, with huge flocks of dunlin in autumn and skies full of tumbling black-and-white lapwing; not to mention the omnipresent, ever-screeching gulls.

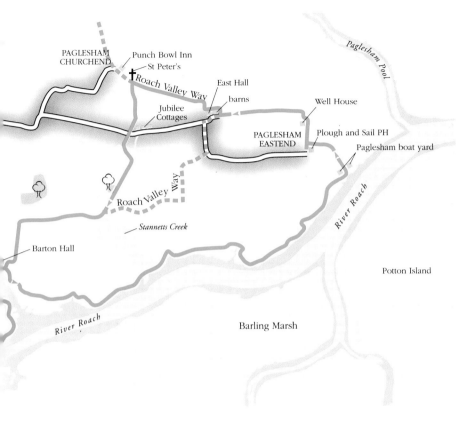

Murderer's home patch

The seawall path makes a big inland loop to encompass the marshy inlet of Bartonhall Creek. On the inner bank stands Barton Hall (913913), around which the path becomes rough and ill-defined – keep amongst the flattened grasses, and away from the tidal inlets and mudflats. Barton Hall is a modest enough farmhouse on a site that boasts a tremendous and tragic toehold in English history. In 1170 Barton Hall was the home of Sir Richard de Brito, a Norman knight keen to please his king. When Henry II delivered himself of his famous outburst, 'Is there none among the cowards that eat my bread who will rid me of this turbulent priest?', de Brito and his three infamous colleagues spurred for Canterbury, where they cut down the troublesome archbishop, Thomas à Becket, in front of his own altar.

Paglesham Eastend

After the lonely, exhilarating miles, the return of civilisation is heralded by the big sheds and cranes of Paglesham boat yard and a rash of yachts at their moorings out in the river. The clank of crane chains and chink of yacht halyards against masts accompany you as you turn inland through the boat yard (947921) and up the potholed lane through the widely scattered houses of Paglesham Eastend. Some are in brick, others are the more traditional black-painted weatherboard. You reach a road, with the excellent Plough and Sail pub on your left (944923). This is a perfect Essex pub: small, weatherboarded, white-painted, with a red-tiled roof; inside it's low, beamy and friendly.

From the pub, turn back right along the lane for 100 yards (100m); where it bends right towards the boat yard keep ahead (yellow arrow on gateway) past a garage, through a wicket gate and on up the left side of a field. Skirt Well House to reach a road (944927). Follow the road for ¹/₂ mile (0.75km) to East Hall (935927), where you turn right along the side of the first barn (concrete FP fingerpost and RVW) on the Roach Valley Way. Follow yellow arrows and RVW markers onto a farm track which doglegs round the back of East Hall. About 50 yards (50m) after it swings right, go left through a gateway (933928 – yellow arrow, RVW) and follow the field edge for ¹/₂ mile (0.75km), then skirt behind some houses to reach St Peter's Church at Paglesham Churchend (926931).

Paglesham Churchend
St Peter's is a rugged old building, its stones eaten into uneven chunks by the winds and weather of flatland Essex. An avenue of pollarded limes leads to the door. The church boasts some nice medieval stone heads: a king, a nun and a queen, all gaping. The charming village of Paglesham Churchend consists of a single short street of houses: white-painted, weatherboarded, with flowers round their doors. At the western end of the street stands the three-storey Punch Bowl pub, white and weatherboarded; inside are dark beams, low ceilings and a warren of nooks and snugs.

'Hard Apple', king of the Essex smugglers
Charm was not one of the chief attributes of the famed and feared William Blyth, king of the area's notorious smugglers during the late 18th century. This clever and savage brigand, known as 'Hard Apple', would munch broken wineglasses and drain a keg of brandy at a sitting, to impress and intimidate foes and friends alike. He once took on a bull in a wrestling match, and threw it to the ground.

Blyth's smuggling cutter *Big Jane* was well known to the excisemen. On one occasion they caught the Churchend gang red-handed, and ordered them to transfer their contraband kegs from *Big Jane* to the excise boat. While Hard Apple engaged the customs captain in a drinking bout below decks, his men found little resistance among the excise crew when they suggested broaching one of the brandy kegs. In no time the King's men were roaring merry, and the illegal kegs were being manhandled by the crafty smugglers back into *Big Jane*'s hold.

Hard Apple was the church warden at St Peter's and found the church tower a very handy hiding place for contraband. The smuggler chief was a grocer by trade, and his customers would often find their purchases wrapped in pages torn from the church registers. Hard Apple died in 1830 aged 84, in the odour of sanctity. On his deathbed he had a chapter of the Bible and the Lord's Prayer read to him, and his last words as he turned his face to the wall were: 'Thank you. Now I'm ready for the launch'.

From the Punch Bowl return to the church. Turn right (concrete FP fingerpost) along a field edge to the road at Jubilee Cottages (926925). Turn right, and in 50 yards (50m) go left through the hedge (concrete FP fingerpost). Follow the path over the field to cross a stream by a metal footbridge. Follow the stream as it bends left (keeping it on your right), then, at its following right bend (926923), look ahead to see two clumps of trees. Near the left edge of the right-hand clump, two high-rise towers are visible in the distance. Aim for these towers across the field, passing the wood edge (924920) and keeping ahead to reach an old flood bank. Keep forward along this to meet the Roach Valley Way and turn right at the top corner of Stannets Creek (923917 – yellow arrow and RVW on post). The RVW skirts the field edge with a hedge on your left, and soon bears left through the hedge to join a farm track. Keep ahead on this track as it bends left (914917) and runs south to Barton Hall.

Rejoin the Roach Valley Way here and turn right along the seawall. In 250 yards (250m) the seawall swings away to the left (909913); keep ahead to join a lane through the farming settlement of Hampton Barns. Pretty Georgian cottages, stables and barns make a harmonious picture. Soon the lane forks; take the left, tarmac fork for ⅔ mile (1km) to reach the road below Great Stambridge. Turn left along the road and pass a lay-by on the right; in 100 yards (100m) turn right (897913 – concrete FP fingerpost) along a field edge with the hedge on your right. At the hedge end keep ahead (yellow arrow on post), and in 200 yards (200m) turn left (893914 – yellow arrow). Keep ahead along field edges to the road by the Cherry Tree pub (890908).

Turn right along the pavement; in 150 yards (150m) turn left along Mill Lane. In 250 yards (250m) bear right (887905 – concrete FP fingerpost) on a field edge under two sets of pylon lines to reach a road, Rocheway (882906), on the eastern outskirts of Rochford. Keep ahead up the road to a T-junction. Turn left along the road, East Street, until it meets South Street (876905). Cross the road and walk along West Street to reach Rochford Station.

SHOREHAM, LULLINGSTONE & EYNSFORD

The River Darent's north–south valley is one of north Kent's most beautiful spots, and the walk from Shoreham to Eynsford and back does it full justice. Here are two castles to enjoy: one a poignant early Norman ruin, the other a handsome Elizabethan house. Shoreham and Eynsford villages boast some very attractive riverside scenes and a clutch of nice old cottages apiece. Shoreham has notable artistic connections with William Blake and Samuel Palmer. There's a remarkable Roman villa at Lullingstone, with the finest mosaic pavement ever unearthed in Kent. Above all, this expedition offers hours of walking through superbly lovely river-valley scenery.

Start & Finish:	Shoreham Station
Length of walk:	8 miles (13km)
OS maps:	1:50,000 Landranger 177, 1:25,000 Explorer 147, 162
Travel:	By rail from London Victoria (50 mins); by road – M25 (Jct 4), A224 south for 1 mile (1.6km), minor road to Shoreham.
Features:	Shoreham village and church; river scenery in Darent Valley; Lullingstone Castle and St Botolph's Church; Lullingstone Roman Villa; Eynsford Castle; Eynsford old bridge and village.
Refreshments:	Ye Olde George Inn, Shoreham; Old Ford Tea Rooms and several pubs in Eynsford.

THE WALK

From Shoreham Station (526615) walk down the station approach, and at the A225 turn right down Station Road ('Shoreham Village' sign) to Shoreham's Church of St Peter and St Paul (523616).

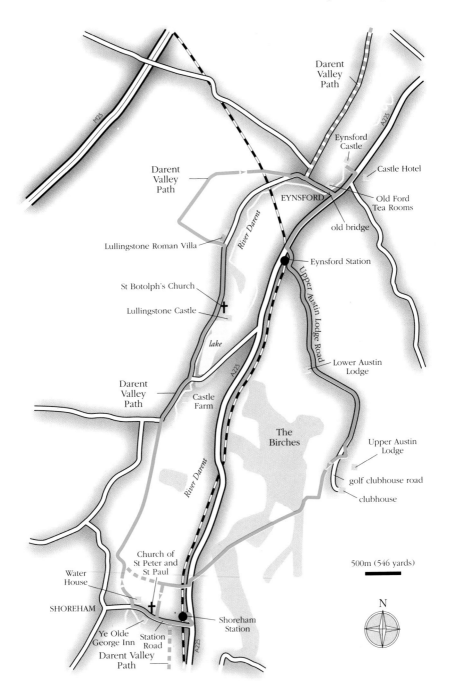

Darent
Valley
Path

Eynsford
Castle

Castle Hotel

Darent
Valley
Path

EYNSFORD

Old Ford
Tea Rooms

old bridge

Lullingstone Roman Villa

River Darent

Eynsford Station

St Botolph's Church

Upper Austin Lodge Road

Lullingstone Castle

lake

Lower Austin
Lodge

A225

Darent
Valley
Path

Castle
Farm

The
Birches

Upper Austin
Lodge

golf clubhouse road

River Darent

clubhouse

500m (546 yards)

Church of
St Peter and
St Paul

Water
House

N

SHOREHAM

Shoreham
Station

Ye Olde
George Inn

Station
Road

Darent Valley
Path

A225

91

Church of St Peter and St Paul, Shoreham

This 14th- and 15th-century village church with its brick-paved yew avenue holds some notable treasures. You enter through an early Tudor south porch hewn from a single mighty oak. Inside on the west wall hangs a lively painting by Charles Cope RA, showing Lt Verney Lovett Cameron of the Royal Navy, son of the vicar of Shoreham, returning to the village church amid enthusiastic scenes after commanding the first European expedition to cross central Africa.

The church boasts a really fine 15th-century rood screen carved with a tangled trail of vine leaves and bunches of grapes. Its top bulges out, braced by superbly carved vaulting; the Rood or great cross would have stood on top in pre-Reformation days. The beautifully carved organ casing came from Westminster Abbey; some say that it encased the organ that Henry Purcell played there.

Water House

From the church continue along the village street, enjoying the handsome old brick houses with their high garden walls and neatly clipped hedges. Just before the bridge, bear right past the war memorial (521616 – 'Darent Valley Path/DVP' fingerpost), and along the left side of Water House. This dignified, square, white-painted house behind its thick evergreen hedge often played host to William Blake (1757–1827), visionary poet and painter. One of the 19th century's best-known English watercolourists, Samuel Palmer (1805–84), stayed at Water House for several years as a member of a group of Blake's followers who styled themselves The Ancients. Palmer began his sojourns here in the year of Blake's death.

From Water House continue along the right bank of the River Darent. In 1/4 mile (0.4km), DVP yellow arrows point left across a footbridge (520621) and on along the left bank of the river. Follow DVP yellow arrows and stiles through the fields of the beautiful Darent Valley for 1 mile (1.6km). You will cross a concrete path, but don't take it. The walk runs past a hop garden with its giant cat's cradle of wooden poles and wires. At the tarmac road (523634 – DVP fingerpost) bear right and keep ahead past Castle Farm and the Hop Shop, where you can buy hop vines, dried flowers and local produce of all sorts. Continue along the road; in 300 yards (300m), at Lullingstone Park Visitor Centre and where the road swings right, keep ahead (526638 – DVP fingerpost) along the river

Opposite: Ducks lurk around the pretty old ford beside the bridge at Eynsford, hoping to persuade passing walkers with a soft spot for feathered friends to share their sandwiches with them.

for ¹/₃ mile (0.5km) to a road (529644). Lullingstone Castle is just ahead on the right.

Lullingstone Castle and St Botolph's Church

Lullingstone Castle is a handsome Tudor country house set on a lake that was created by damming the River Darent. The approach runs through the arch of a 15th-century brick gatehouse, which perfectly frames the house. The Peche family held the estate from 1361; since Tudor times it has been in the possession of the Hart family, styled Hart-Dyke since the Harts and the Dykes joined in marriage in the mid-18th century. A tour of the castle puts you in touch with intimate family history: portraits of the Harts with their long, intelligent faces and broad cheekbones persisting across 500 years; a poignant likeness of a tiny Hart boy (he died in childhood), still in skirts, clutching a bunch of cherries; the helmet worn by Tudor jousting champion Sir John Hart at the Field of the Cloth of Gold in 1520. There is also the grandeur attached to an ancient and influential family: the magnificent Elizabethan plasterwork in the barrel-vaulted ceiling of the first-floor state drawing room; the great staircase inserted to flatter Queen Anne on her visit here and the elaborately carved bed provided for her.

To one side of the house stands St Botolph's Church. It's well worth glancing round the interior. The Flemish rood screen of 1500–1520 is heavily carved with Tudor roses, foliage and peach stones ('pêche'), and the windows are filled with stained glass that ranges from willowy 14th-century saints in green robes to Tudor yellow-and-white roundels that include Jesus crucified on a vine shoot. There's a beautiful plaster ceiling, and the tomb of Sir George and Lady Elizabeth Hart guarded by cherubs with a spade and a skull, an angel with a laurel wreath, and a ghoulish shrouded skeleton. Also here is Sir Percyvall Hart, one of Queen Anne's principal courtiers (hence the queen's visit to Lullingstone). It is said that Sir Percyvall's daughter, Ann, jilted her fiancé, Sir Thomas Dyke, during their engagement party, sliding from her chamber window down a knotted-sheet rope to elope with and marry her lover, a naval officer named Bluet. After Bluet's death nine years later, however, Ann found the faithful Sir Thomas still willing, and they were finally joined in marriage.

From the castle, continue along the tarmac track for ¹/₃ mile (0.5km), to reach Lullingstone Roman Villa on your left (530651).

Lullingstone Roman Villa

The protective building that covers the Roman villa could qualify for the title of 'Kent's Ugliest', but the villa itself – unearthed on the west bank of the River Darent in 1939 – is Kent's finest. This splendid dwelling, built first in timber around AD 75, but later solidly rebuilt in flint cobbles and tiles, was preserved for posterity by the lucky accident of its location, at the foot of a steep slope. Over the centuries, soil washed down the hill, and covered the villa remains with an earthy, protective blanket.

Nearly 30 rooms are clustered together in a nest of flint-walled spaces. They include cellars, a bath house, bedrooms, a kitchen, verandahs and living rooms. On the walls of a 4th-century chapel the excavators found fragments of decorated plaster which, when pieced together, revealed figures of Christians praying. Also decorating the walls was a Christian 'Chi-Ro' or Christ monogram. Older faiths were also practised at Lullingstone: witness the niche painting in the well cellar, depicting a water goddess with water flowing from her nipples and reeds sprouting from her hair.

Of all the artefacts on display, the chief treasure is the wonderful mosaic pavement laid in the floor of the dining room-cum-audience chamber. The lower panel shows a graceful, naked Europa being abducted by a rampant Jupiter in bull shape (a winged cupid grabs the bull by the tail in a vain attempt to slow things down). The upper panel depicts a red-cloaked Bellerophon astride Pegasus (the winged horse), his right hand stabbing a long lance through the back of a not-very-threatening chimera. This panel also contains some jolly, bulging sea beasts, and has at its corners three of the four seasons (summer is missing). A riot of geometrical symbols fills the space between the two panels, including swastikas, triangles, hearts and shaded crosses. The contrast between the formality of the geometrical designs and the free-flowing expressionism of the classical panels is breathtaking. This is certainly one of the finest pieces of Roman art discovered in Britain.

From the villa, return along the track for 10 yards (10m) to the Lullingstone Castle entrance; bear right here up steps (DVP arrow and 'Lullingstone Park Circular Walk' fingerpost). Climb the path by the field edge; at the top of the field turn right to cross a stile (525652 – DVP yellow arrow on a post) and follow a hedge on your right. In ¹/₃ mile (0.5km) cross a tarmac track and continue down a field to cross the railway on the level (533657). Continue down across the next field to reach the road in Eynsford. Keep forward round a right bend. In 20 yards (20m) the DVP turns left, but keep ahead here (537657 – 'Eynsford' sign) to reach the A225. Turn left here. Opposite the Castle Hotel, turn left ('Village Hall' sign) down an alley to find Eynsford Castle (542658).

Eynsford Castle

Eynsford is a charming village, full of attractive old brick and weatherboarded houses, many with photogenic clusters of tall chimneys and over-sailing upper storeys. The castle was one of the first built in stone by the Normans, a great many-sided stronghold that was never strengthened by the addition of battlements. The castle builders evidently expected things to be peaceful among the subdued tribes of the Darent Valley. The flint walls stand 30 feet (9m) tall; there are archways, doors and windows, and the remnants of a 12th-century dwelling within the rugged, gloomy, grey ruins.

From the castle return to the A225 and turn right to walk the length of the village (pavements all the way). Just before the road goes under the railway bridge (536650), bear left past Eynsford Station and continue along Upper Austin Lodge Road for 1½ miles (2.5km) to reach Upper Austin Lodge. The Austin Valley is a beautiful side cleft off the Darent Valley, its chalky fields swooping and rolling like immense, smooth sea billows. There is an old wooden oast and a working forge at Lower Austin Lodge, and a valley road that peters out ¾ mile (1.2km) further up at Upper Austin Lodge. Apart from the rattle of trains on the nearby railway line there are few sounds to disturb the peace of this delectable 'lost valley'.

The road passes through the gates of Upper Austin Lodge (542637). It soon divides; take the left fork ('Private Road, No Entry' sign). In 100 yards (100m) bear right over a stile (542631 – yellow arrow and 'Footpath to Shoreham' sign). Cross the golf course clubhouse road and continue along the valley bottom with a hedge on your left. At the end of the second field turn right between hedges (539627) and climb the valley slope to turn left inside the bottom edge of a wood. In 150 yards (150m) the track bears right and climbs steps to leave the wood just short of the crest of the ridge (537625). Keep forward here on a grass track, steering a little left to enter a wood (534624). NB Although the OS Explorer and Landranger maps both show a rifle range here, it is no longer used.

The path forks immediately; take the left-hand path. In ⅓ mile (0.5km), at another fork (530622), a yellow arrow on a post points right. This path soon dips steeply downhill, past a flagpole and on down. At the foot of the slope leave the trees and cross a house drive. 'Footpath' signs direct you along another woodland footpath, then across a field to meet the A225 (527619). Cross the road (with great care!) and turn left for 60 yards (60m), then right (FP fingerpost and DVP post) to cross the railway – listen carefully for trains – by stiles. Keep forward down the field with the hedge on your left. At the end of the hedge turn left (524619 – yellow arrow) along the field bottom to the road in Shoreham (523615). Turn left to reach Shoreham Station.

TEYNHAM, CONYER & THE SWALE

Moody, muddy and magnificent – that sums up the character of this fine walk through the North Kent apple orchards and along the banks of the broad Swale, the tidal channel that separates the Kentish mainland from the Isle of Sheppey. Beautiful at any time of year, maximum enjoyment comes in spring (apple-blossom time) or autumn (fruit harvest); though winter is wonderful along the Swale too, if you are well wrapped up, thanks to the multitudes of overwintering wildfowl that throng the channel. There are two fine churches to enjoy en route (you'll need to plan ahead to get St Mary's, Teynham, unlocked – see Further Information, pages 192–201), and one of the best pubs in Kent, the darkly atmospheric Ship Inn at Conyer.

Start & Finish:	Teynham Station
Length of walk:	10½ miles (17km)
OS maps:	1:50,000 Landranger 178; 1:25,000 Explorer 149
Travel:	By rail from London Victoria (1 hr 20 mins); by road – M25 (Jct 2), M2 (Jct 5), A249 to Sittingbourne, A2 to Teynham.
Features:	Orchard landscape; Ship Inn, Conyer; bird-watching along the Swale (don't forget your binoculars!); St Mary's Church, Luddenham; St Mary's Church, Teynham.
Refreshments:	Ship Inn, Conyer; Three Mariners PH or Castle Free House, Oare.

THE WALK

From the platform at Teynham Station (957631) bear left over the bridge, descending to a lane that leads into open fields. Walk to a row of cottages ahead and take the footpath that runs in front of them. Continue along a green lane, which in 100 yards (100m) turns right (956632) to run between a sewage works and allotments. Soon a hedge comes in on your right; keep it there for ½ mile (0.75km) as you walk north-north-east through orchards.

Fruit and malaria

The silt and clay of these North Kent soils, combined with the mildness of the climate, make this excellent country for fruit growing. Although many of the orchards have been grubbed out in recent years and replaced by grassland or arable fields, much of the flat country hereabouts is still given over to stumpy apple, pear and cherry trees. When the pink or green–white flush of spring blossom is on these acres of geometrically drilled fruit trees the effect is stunning.

Cherries were first cultivated in the region by Richard Harrys, one of the Tudor era's most green-fingered and forward-looking experts. Harrys was fruiterer to His (extremely demanding) Majesty King Henry VIII, so it was important to get things right if head retention was on the agenda. The royal fruiterer planted 105 acres (about 40ha) with cherry trees imported from Flanders, and the area never looked back. Teynham became southern England's centre of fruit growing in Tudor times, famous for 'the sweet Cherry, the temperate Pipyn'. The trade continued to flourish through succeeding centuries, and the most senior locals can still remember the red-sailed cherry barges that would carry the fruit to Covent Garden and other London markets.

But things were not always so smooth and prosperous around Teynham. Only just north of the village stretched the freshwater marshes, reclaimed from the sea, where stagnant puddles of water provided perfect breeding grounds for malarial mosquitoes. 'He that will not live long, Let him dwell at Murston, Teynham or Tonge,' warned the local doggerel. Medieval Teynham was notorious for its exaggerated rate of death from 'marsh ague' or malaria. Part of the problem arose from the construction of seawalls along the Kentish shoreline – begun by the Romans and continued by the medieval monastic communities – which not only strengthened the area's sea defences and increased its value for agriculture, but also encouraged the development of malarial marshes. The Roman shoreline had run just inland of the present-day one, and the Romans tended vineyards on terraced slopes here. But by the late Middle Ages the populace had been forced to move inland to healthier areas.

Where the hedge on your right comes to an end, bear slightly left to cross a footbridge (961642) and follow the left bank of a reedy ditch beneath power lines and on to the road in Conyer (963645). Turn left here along the dead-end road 'The Quay', following Swale Heritage Trail (SHT) markers, to reach the Ship Inn at the end of the road (961648).

Opposite: When you reach the Swale seawall path take the time to pause and enjoy the wide views across creeks and saltings.

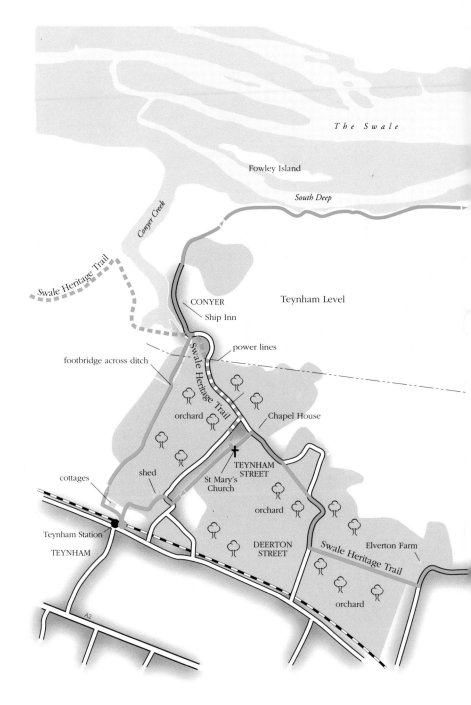

The Swale

Fowley Island

South Deep

Conyer Creek

Swale Heritage Trail

CONYER

Ship Inn

Teynham Level

power lines

Swale Heritage Trail

footbridge across ditch

orchard

Chapel House

TEYNHAM
STREET

cottages

shed

St Mary's
Church

orchard

Teynham Station

TEYNHAM

DEERTON
STREET

Swale Heritage Trail

Elverton Farm

orchard

A2

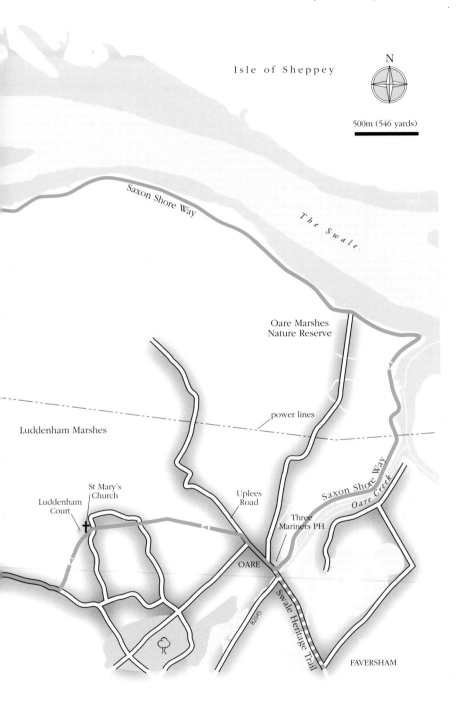

Isle of Sheppey

N

500m (546 yards)

Saxon Shore Way

The Swale

Oare Marshes
Nature Reserve

power lines

Luddenham Marshes

Saxon Shore Way

Oare Creek

St Mary's
Church

Luddenham
Court

Uplees
Road

Three
Mariners PH

OARE

Swale Heritage Trail

B2045

FAVERSHAM

Conyer and the Ship Inn

In Victorian times Conyer was a little brick-making port, sending bricks out by barges loaded up at the wharf in the mouth of Conyer Creek. Conyer was one of a thousand maritime or estuarine villages around the coasts of Britain that maintained a life-blood of coastal commerce from their little wharves, jetties or quays. Railways, and then road transport, along with the gradual silting up of these muddy outlets, put an end to a hugely diverse, small-scale commercial trade. Conyer's Ship Inn is a throwback to those more leisurely days – an end-of-the-road inn out on a limb; dark, firelit and friendly; a pub with books in its bar and great local conversation round its tables – you'll find it hard to tear yourself away.

From the Ship Inn, a path on the right of the pub leads across rough ground, partially paved with old Conyer bricks, to the seawall path along the Swale (966655). Direction-finding is easy for the next 5 miles (8km): just follow the path east to the mouth of Oare Creek (018646), then turn right and walk inland along the creek to Oare village.

Bird-watching along the Swale

The Swale is the swirling, tidal channel that separates the Isle of Sheppey from the shore of north Kent. Rather more than a mile wide here, the Swale was a formidable obstacle before the first Kingsferry Bridge was built in the 1860s. Ferry boats were the only way of getting on and off the island, and during this section of the walk you pass the sites of two of them: Elmley Ferry where you join the seawall path, and Harty Ferry at the far end of the Swale. The Sheppey shore seems low and dark as you look across the water. Nearer at hand you pass Fowley Island ('island of fowl'), where you may spot owls or harriers. The creeks and mudflats of the Swale provide a wonderfully rich larder for wildfowl; regulars include curlews, redshanks, oystercatchers, turnstones, grebes and lapwings, with big crowds of brent geese, dunlins and wigeons in season. You might see plovers, shelducks and teals, ragged grey herons and sleek deadly sparrowhawks. Binoculars are a walker's best friend here. It's no wonder that the Swale has been declared a site of international importance for overwintering wildfowl.

Explosion on the marshes

In the 19th century Oare Marshes were reclaimed largely for the purpose of building a big explosives factory. The manufacture of guncotton began here around 1870, quickly followed by other explosives including nitroglycerine, cordite and TNT. The chickens came home to roost, however, in the middle of World War I – on 2 April 1916, 165 tons of TNT and ammunition blew up with a concussion that was felt nearly 100 miles (165km) away in Norwich.

One hundred and sixteen workers died in this, the worst munitions explosion in British history. Production of explosives stopped after the war. In the 1960s local conservationists defeated a plan to turn the marshes into a marina, and they are now administered as a nature reserve – exactly the destiny one would have hoped to see them fulfil.

From the seawall path turn right along Oare's main street to pass the Three Mariners pub. In 250 yards (250m) keep ahead down Uplees Road for 30 yards (30m), then turn left over a stile (004630 – SHT marker), and walk diagonally across the fields to cross a lane (997631). From here, aim straight between the oast towers and the church tower at Luddenham Court, to reach St Mary's Church (992631).

Luddenham Court and St Mary's Church

When medieval Luddenham Court was built, the area was probably still tidal, with the sea washing twice daily up against the low ridge on which the farmstead stands. Together with the big oasts for drying hops, the barns and the outbuildings, house and church form a tranquil, nucleated ensemble that can hardly have changed over the passing centuries.

Luddenham Court is private property, but the owners run a farm shop where you can pick up the key for the church. The red-brick tower was put up in 1866 to replace one that tumbled down, but the main body of the little church is essentially Norman, with some thin Roman tiles reused to fortify the walls. It's a plain interior, stripped of its pews, entered through a low round-headed doorway. On the nave floor by the font lies a cracked Purbeck marble coffin lid of the 14th century, carved in high relief with a cross and two hands raising a chalice – or perhaps it's a crown.

From the church follow the plentiful SHT markers across the fields to a road (991626). Turn right along the road for ¾ mile (1.2km). At the entrance to Elverton Farm (981628), follow the road round a left bend. In 150 yards (150m) turn right (SHT sign) for ½ mile (0.75km) on a path along the edges of orchards. Quarter of a mile (0.4km) along the path cross over a concrete road, keeping a tall evergreen hedge to your left. At Deerton Street turn right along a road (972629), which soon bends left. Just beyond the following right bend, go left over a stile (972633 – SHT sign) and keep a hedge on your left to reach a road. Keep forward through Teynham Street. Opposite Chapel House turn left over a stile (968638 – FP fingerpost and SHT sign) to Teynham's St Mary's Church.

St Mary's Church, Teynham

The large cruciform church – 12th century in origin, though what one sees today is largely 13th-century work – seems curiously imposing for its isolated position among a handful of scattered farms. This 'Cathedral of the Orchards' was built to reflect the glory of the archbishops of Canterbury, who had a palace just to the west of the church. Many archbishops spent a good deal of their year here in medieval times.

The exterior of the church under its 15th-century tower looks rugged and weather-beaten. The rough walls contain slivers of Roman tiles. You enter through a fine 15th-century oak door which contains several deep bullet holes; the shots were fired by Roundheads who were besieging a party of Royalists barricaded in the church after a nearby Civil War skirmish. Inside the church a short length of wide-link chain is fixed low down in the south wall; local legend says that Oliver Cromwell attached his horse to it while stabling the beast in the church.

In spite of its size, St Mary's has a homely feel, perhaps because of the criss-cross of rafter-like beams in the roof and the two lattice-panel clerestory windows, high in the south wall, that would better suit a domestic setting. Under the choir floor carpet you'll find a brass to William and Elizabeth Palmer (1639), both in handsome Stuart dress. The north transept carpet conceals a small-scale brass to William Wreke (1533) in a merchant's robe, and another to Robert Heyward (1620) and to two children: one a long-haired boy, the other a baby tightly wrapped in swaddling clothes. Under the south transept carpet is a splendid brass to a fully armoured John Frogenhall, his feet resting on a faithful dog.

Leave St Mary's by the lychgate and walk along the lane. In 25 yards (25m), where the lane bends right, keep ahead (965636) on a fenced path through orchards and rough ground to meet a road (961633). Turn right for 100 yards (100m), then left into a farmyard to bear left along the front of a big corrugated shed. Walk along a driveway ('pedestrian' sign). In 150 yards (150m) turn right along a fence (959632). In 100 yards (100m) the path turns left between fences to reach Teynham Station.

HOLLINGBOURNE, NORTH DOWNS WAY & THURNHAM

Four miles (6km) of exhilarating downland tramping along the North Downs Way (NDW) form the backbone of this walk, and the views from the crest of the downs are truly stunning. Hollingbourne is a charming village, its street lined with handsome old houses. The Elizabethan mansion of Hollingbourne Manor was home for centuries to the Colepepers, an eminent Kent family, and All Saints' Church contains many memorials to them. It's worth seeking out the unique and beautiful Colepeper Cloth, a genuine labour of love. At Thurnham you can pay your respects at the grave of the Mighty Mynn, one of the titans of 19th-century Kent cricket.

Start & Finish:	Hollingbourne Station
Length of walk:	8 miles (13km)
OS maps:	1:50,000 Landranger 188; 1:25,000 Explorer 148
Travel:	By rail from London Victoria (1 hr 15 mins); by road – M25 (Jct 5 or 4), M20 (Jct 8), A20 towards Lenham for ½ mile (0.75km), left to Hollingbourne.
Features:	Old houses in Hollingbourne; Colepeper Cloth; Colepeper and Gethin monuments in All Saints' Church, Hollingbourne; views south from North Downs Way; Mighty Mynn memorial at the Church of St Mary the Virgin, Thurnham.
Refreshments:	Dirty Habit PH, Hollingbourne; Black Horse PH, Thurnham.

THE WALK

From Hollingbourne Station (834551) walk down the long station approach. Turn left under the railway; in 150 yards (150m) turn left (840549 – FP fingerpost) along a footpath to All Saints' Church in Hollingbourne (843551).

Hollingbourne's famous trencherman

There are several very fine medieval houses in Hollingbourne, a village which seems to have been passed over by the outside world. But it attracted a tabloid-style fame in the early 17th-century because of the eating habits of one of its residents, Nicholas Wood. He was a famous trencherman, who once entered a wager to eat at one sitting as much black pudding as would stretch across the River Thames between London and Richmond. Wood's obsession with eating went far beyond such stunts, though. Contemporary reports say that he would 'devour at one meal what was provided for twenty men, eat a whole hog at a sitting, and at another time thirty dozen of pigeons'. The poor man was obviously suffering from a rampaging eating disorder. Medical men of the time named it 'caninus appetitus', Hound's Hunger. Wood died a pauper in 1630, having spent all he possessed on food.

All Saints' Church, Hollingbourne

In All Saints' Church you'll find several monuments to the Colepeper family of Hollingbourne Manor. The most striking is in the north chapel, dedicated to the family, with 124 stone heraldic shields on the walls (only two still retain their painted devices) and the centrally placed white marble effigy of Lady Elizabeth Colepeper who died in 1638 aged 56, 'the best of women, the best of wives, the best of mothers'. Her feet rest on a freakish-looking animal, snub-nosed and snarling, with a dog's head, leopard's spots, a cow's tail and cloven hooves: a 'thoye', one of medieval heraldry's more curious beasts. On the north chancel wall is a memorial to Sir John Colepeper, a brave Royalist who fought at the battles of Naseby and Keinton, and went into exile with the king-in-waiting, Charles II.

The Colepeper Cloth

While Sir John was in exile his four daughters embroidered what is known as the Colepeper Cloth – perhaps as an altar cloth, or maybe as a pall for a coffin. It took the young women 12 years and cost one of them her eyesight, ruined through so many hours of close work by candlelight. The cloth is not on public show, but can be viewed by prior arrangement. It is a beautiful work, a 6-foot- (2-m-) long rectangle of purple velvet surrounded by a broad border of Kentish fruits worked in coloured dyes and gold thread: acorns, cobnuts, pears and plums, pomegranates with star-like flowers, mulberries and quinces, peaches and grapes. All these

Opposite: The North Downs Way runs as a well-marked track across the south-facing flanks of the hills above Thurnham.

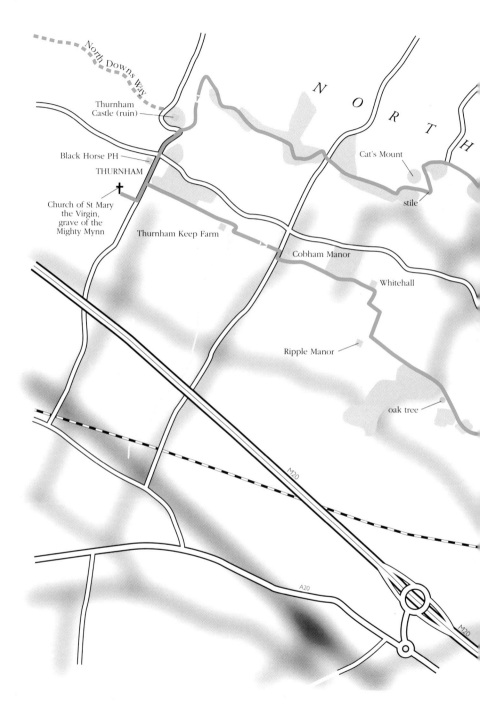

North Downs Way

Thurnham
Castle (ruin)

Black Horse PH

THURNHAM

Church of St Mary
the Virgin,
grave of the
Mighty Mynn

Thurnham Keep Farm

N O R T H

Cat's Mount

stile

Cobham Manor

Whitehall

Ripple Manor

oak tree

M20

A20

M20

HUCKING

D O W N S

North Downs Way

BROAD STREET

Pilgrims' Way

N

500m (546 yards)

Hollingbourne Manor

HOLLINGBOURNE

Dirty Habit PH

Hollingbourne Station

North Downs Way

EYHORNE STREET

bridge

All Saints' Church

Pilgrims' Way

were embroidered onto coarse linen, then stitched to the work with gold thread. A border of angels separates the inner rectangle of velvet from the frame of fruit, and another angel border follows the outer edge of the piece. It is a remarkable and moving work of art, and a testament to daughterly devotion.

From the church, walk through the lychgate and turn left up the road, passing the big brick-built Tudor house of Hollingbourne Manor and continuing up the village street. Pass over the crossroads above the Dirty Habit pub, and in 50 yards (50m) bear left (845554 – NDW fingerpost) up steps and along a path among trees, then along a field edge to go through a kissing gate. A NDW yellow arrow and acorn symbol points out the path, climbing open ground diagonally left to a post seen above. Turn left here (847557 – yellow arrow) along a track for 200 yards (200m); pass through a kissing gate and continue, gaining height on a snaking track to the top of the downs.

Ancient trackways of the North Downs

The North Downs Way National Trail shadows the course of the Pilgrims' Way, the medieval pilgrim path from Winchester to the shrine of St Thomas à Becket at Canterbury. The pilgrims themselves were treading in the footsteps of travellers who had beaten out the ancient trackway over 5,000 years: drovers, then merchants, warriors and others. The old road kept just below the crest of the downs on their southward side, a course that afforded shelter from the weather, a grandstand lookout, and concealment from the eyes of potential enemies. From the North Downs Way you enjoy a largely uninterrupted southward panorama over 30 or 40 miles (50–70km) of rolling, beautiful Wealden country, thickly wooded, with a blue line of hills closing the far horizon.

These long scrubby grassland slopes provide a wonderful chalky habitat for lime-loving plants: wild thyme, cowslips, salad burnet, marjoram, and a number of beautiful orchids. Chalkhill blue butterflies flitter over the slopes, which are grazed by sheep; grazing and scrub control are vital components in the jigsaw of management of this Area of Outstanding Natural Beauty.

The North Downs Way continues north-west along the crest of the downs, passing under power lines (843565) to reach a T-junction of tracks (842567) at a Hucking Estate notice. Turn left here for 100 yards (100m), then right (NDW yellow arrow) and on through trees for ½ mile (0.75km). At OS grid reference 836581 you cross a lane (FP fingerpost). In 200 yards (200m) the NDW crosses a stile and turns left downhill for 100 yards (100m), then bears right for 100 yards (100m) to turn right through a hedge at a post with a yellow arrow (832583). Ignore the well-marked track that runs to the left along the contour, aim a little higher instead to cross a stile halfway up the near edge of a scrub wood (NDW arrow). Follow NDW markers through scrubby trees for ½ mile (0.75km) to join a muddy bridleway. Follow it downhill out of the trees as it swings south round Cat's Mount. Watch out for the NDW arrow on a post on the left of the track; turn right over a stile here (825577), climb to cross another stile and keep on up between a yew grove and a fence. Continue for ½ mile (0.75km), descending steps to cross a lane (818578 – NDW fingerpost). Keep ahead along the North Downs Way, ignoring the FP fingerpost on the left in 50 yards (50m).

In ⅓ mile (0.5km), the North Downs Way turns off to the left (816580 – NDW arrow), descending and then ascending steps. Continue for ⅓ mile (0.5km) to leave the trees over a stile (812582). Keep a fence on your left, climbing a slope to turn left and descend into the head of a dry valley. Go left over a stile here (NDW arrow) and follow the path down the right side of the valley. At a road (868580) leave the North Downs Way and turn left downhill into Thurnham. Pass the Black Horse pub (806579), and in 300 yards (300m) turn right along a path (805576 – 'St Mary's Church' fingerpost) to the Church of St Mary the Virgin.

The Mighty Mynn

On the north side of St Mary's, the Mighty Mynn rests under a yew tree. Alfred Mynn (1807–61), the 'Lion of Kent', was a genuine 19th-century cricket hero, a 17-stone (108-kg) round-arm fast bowler and ferocious batsman. He was born at Goudhurst, but lived for many years in Thurnham. With the ball the Mighty Mynn could 'maintain a terrific pace for hours without fatigue'. With the bat he was a whirlwind. In 1836 he made four consecutive scores of 283 – two of these not out.

The Lion of Kent was a man with open hands and a big heart, according to his memorial stone: 'His kindness of heart and generosity of disposition during many years of public life as the Champion of English cricketers endeared him to a large circle of admiring friends. His widespread popularity is attested by the circumstance that four hundred persons have united to erect this tombstone, and to found in honour of a name so celebrated the Mynn Memorial Benevolent Institution for Kentish Cricketers.'

From the church return up the road. In 150 yards (150m) turn right (805577 – FP fingerpost) along a lane to Thurnham Keep Farm. Pass the twin oasts and follow yellow arrows over a stile and along a field edge with a fence on your left to cross a stile into a road (815572) at Cobham Manor.

Turn right for 50 yards (50m); just past a weatherboarded oast house, turn left (FP fingerpost in the hedge) through a gate and across the oast-house courtyard; then across three stiles in quick succession. Pass through a gate, then up steps in a bank and over a stile (816572 – yellow arrow). Keep ahead with a fence on your right, over a stile and down a slope, bearing a little left to cross a stile and go through a gate in a belt of trees (yellow arrow). Continue with the hedge on your left to cross another stile (820570 – yellow arrow). Keep ahead across scrubby ground for 20 yards (20m) to cross another stile and walk along a fenced path to Whitehall, where you go through two wicket gates to a road (821570 – PB fingerpost).

Turn right along the road. It doglegs left, then right. In another 150 yards (150m) turn left at a 'Ripple Manor' sign (821567 – yellow arrow on post) along a field edge and up the left side of a wood. At the wood end (826563 – yellow arrow) aim diagonally right for a lone oak tree, then continue to the left corner of the wood beyond (827561 – yellow arrow on post).

Field path back to Hollingbourne

The return route along field paths through the low valley landscape makes an enjoyable contrast to the previous high-level striding along the North Downs Way. All around are vast hedgeless fields, farms like little settlements with their cottages and converted oasts, and blocks of woodland that break up the broad arable vistas.

From the wood's corner, aim for the right corner of a short strip of trees, and from here bear left to the bottom right corner of the wood ahead (829560 – yellow arrow on post). From here, aim diagonally right across the field; once over the ridge, make for the short yellow-topped post seen ahead (831557). Turn right along the wood edge, then down the right side of the wood beyond. Keep ahead (831555 – post with yellow arrow), following a clear path to the bottom left corner of the field. Turn left (832552 – yellow arrow) over a plank bridge and up the field edge. In 100 yards (100m) turn right across the railway through kissing gates. On the far side turn left along the hedge; in 150 yards (150m) bear left over a stile and along a path to Hollingbourne Station.

CHARING, LITTLE CHART & PLUCKLEY

The generous spirit of Uncle Silas and Pop Larkin, those nod-and-a-wink Kentish rogues, seems to hang around the apple orchards and lush pastures along this walk. No wonder, since their creator H. E. Bates lived in the idyllic hamlet of Little Chart Forstal, and drew his inspiration from the people and the intimate, small-scale landscape of the Low Weald. There are the remains of the Archbishop's Palace to enjoy at Charing, and ghost tales galore at Pluckley; also, a poignant reminder of the 'doodlebug' attacks of World War II and beautiful woodland both young and old.

Start & Finish:	Charing Station
Length of walk:	9 miles (14km)
OS maps:	1:50,000 Landranger 189; 1:25,000 Explorer 137
Travel:	By rail from London Victoria (1 hr 20 mins); by road – M25 (Jct 5), M26, M20 (Jct 8), A20 to Charing.
Features:	Archbishop's Palace remains, Church of St Peter and St Paul and nice old houses at Charing; plantations and old woods around Honeywood Rough; Little Chart Forstal; ghost tales, Dering brasses in St Nicholas's Church and 'arched windows' at Pluckley; ruins of St Mary's Church, Little Chart.
Refreshments:	Royal Oak PH, Charing; Swan PH, Little Chart; Black Horse PH, Pluckley.

THE WALK

From Charing Station (950491) turn left along Station Road to the village centre. Cross the A20 by the Queen's Head pub and keep ahead up the High Street. Turn right by 'Glen Kirton, Butcher and Baker', to reach the Archbishop's Palace next to the Church of St Peter and St Paul (954494).

Archbishop's Palace, Charing

The visible remains of the sumptuous 14th-century palace of the archbishop of Canterbury are a couple of ancient houses joined by sturdy flint walls, many of their arches and windows filled in with brick and stone, and a great gateway giving a vista through stone arches of a tall, handsome medieval house. In May 1520, King Henry VIII, travelling to France for his historic meeting with the French king François I at the Field of the Cloth of Gold, spent the night here. Many of the 4,000 retainers that the king brought with him feasted in a splendid banqueting hall, which later became the barn you can see alongside the house today.

Church of St Peter and St Paul, Charing

The Church of St Peter and St Paul was built to replace a 13th-century church burned in a freak accident in 1590. A red-hot bullet fired at a pigeon on the roof missed its mark and set the dry wooden shingles alight; the fire destroyed much of the building and melted the bells. The current church has a Tudor roof painted with elaborate curlicues. Two fine brass chandeliers hang low from its beams – 'Kentish Spiders', according to the church notes. The hard wooden pew seats are softened by runners or carpet-like cushions embroidered with motifs that include fish, cats, church bells, local flowers, scenes of primitive husbandry and a fine Four Seasons.

Return from the church to Charing Station and cross the railway bridge. Turn immediately left (FP fingerpost) past houses. Greensand Way Link Route (GWLR) yellow arrow waymarks on a post direct you on with a hedge on your left. Cross a stile; GWLR arrows point diagonally across gates and stiles as the path passes a slaughterhouse (954487). At the end of the third field you have to negotiate a swamp of mud: keep ahead here on the same line over a stile. About 200 yards (200m) along the next field, bear left through the gateway and continue down the field to cross two stiles in the bottom right corner (GWLR arrow). Keep forward here with the woodland of Honeywood Rough on your right.

Low Weald landscape

As soon as you leave Charing the character of the Low Weald landscape becomes clear – broad fields among abundant woods and streams; low hills humped in waves on the southern horizon; a spatter of horse and cattle ponds interspersed with hammer ponds, remnants of the Weald's

Opposite: The present-day archbishop of Canterbury still has use of the 14th-century Archbishop's Palace at Charing, where King Henry VIII and 4,000 followers were entertained in 1520.

medieval iron industry. The woodland hereabouts is particularly beautiful; for example, Honeywood Rough with its old hazel coppice and field maples (brilliant gold in the autumn), and the young groves of aspen, ash, maple and sweet chestnut round which the path threads its way.

Soon the path doglegs left, then right (954480) past a grove. In 150 yards (150m) turn left over a footbridge and stiles (954478); bear diagonally right across the next field to a stile, then to another stile into a road. Keep forward to cross over a railway cutting and continue past Hollybush Farm to cross the M20 motorway (955471). Bear immediately left over a stile, then right (FP fingerpost) to a gate gap in the hedge beside a small wood (955468). Bear diagonally left across the next field. Aim for the farm buildings of The Mount; as soon as you are over the ridge, aim for the gate seen below in the far hedge (956464). Yellow arrows point you on across a stile and up the right side of plant nursery fields. In 100 yards (100m) bear right to cross The Mount's drive by stiles; aim half left to cross a stile behind a gorse clump, and turn right along a road (959462). In 400 yards (400m) turn right across a ditch and stile (958458 – FP fingerpost); follow the path diagonally left over the field to Ram Lane where you turn right into Little Chart Forstal.

Little Chart Forstal and H. E. Bates

'Forstal' seems to signify a village green, an open space cleared from the forest. This particular forstal is an idyllic one, a little cricket ground overlooked by beautiful old houses, some in brick, some in stone, some weatherboarded. Along its south side a wall connects a drum-shaped stone oast or hop-drying kiln, the old dwelling of Coldham, a chunky barn with slit windows and a fine house with a deep porch hood, tile-hung walls and tall chimneys. Here lived the novelist and country writer H. E. Bates. Steeped in the peaceful rural atmosphere of Little Chart Forstal, it's small wonder that bucolic, quintessentially English characters such as the Larkins and Uncle Silas came to inhabit Bates's imagination.

Pass the cricket pitch and turn right (951458 – Greensand Way/GW and Stour Valley Walk/SVW fingerposts) to pass 'Thatch' house. Bear left round its garden (GW and SVW yellow arrows), cross a stile and continue with a hedge on your left to cross another stile. Cross a field to the bottom left corner, where you turn right along the road into Little Chart.

Opposite the welcoming and characterful Swan pub, climb steps and walk past the west or tower end of the red-brick church (944458). This church was built in 1955 as a substitute for Little Chart's medieval church of St Mary, which was destroyed by a flying bomb during World War II (see below). In 100 yards (100m) bear right along a track past a post with a

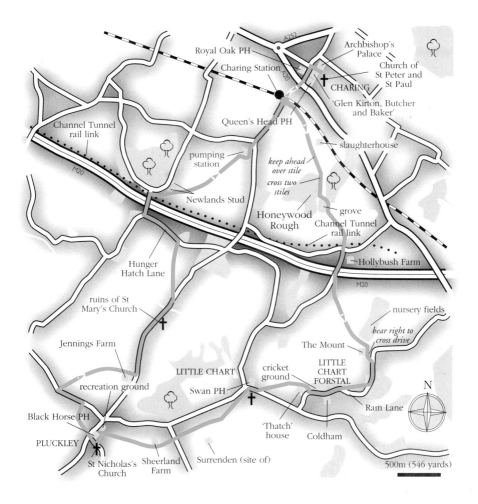

GW yellow arrow. Follow GW waymarks on past orchards and above the site of Surrenden (938453 – see below), to cross a lane (936454). Keep the same line past Sheerland Farm (934454) and more orchards to reach Pluckley recreation ground (927454). Bear left through a gate and the churchyard lychgate to reach St Nicholas's Church.

Strange tales at the 'Most Haunted Village In England'

Keep a lookout for the Red Lady who wanders St Nicholas's churchyard searching for her lost child; also for the gypsy watercress woman who burned to death when her pipe set fire to her shawl, the schoolmaster who hanged himself, the miller and the monk, the highwayman transfixed by a sword, and the fife and drum band that marches through the village houses. Pluckley claims the title of 'Most Haunted Village In England', so you have a fair chance of seeing 'summat strange'.

The Red Lady was a member of the Dering family, occupiers of the house site at Surrenden for 30 generations. You'll see the family crest of a black horse on the commemorative Dering brasses in the south chapel of St Nicholas's Church, on the cowls of oasts (such as the one at Little Chart Forstal) and in the name of Pluckley's pub, the Black Horse (yes, it has a poltergeist!). The Black Horse pub has distinctively shaped windows, like many of the houses in and around Pluckley; they have a rounded upper edge, giving them the look of eyes with brows arched in surprise. Sir Edward Cholmeley Dering (squire of Pluckley throughout the 19th century, having inherited the estate at the age of three) caused the design to be used on so many local houses. He did so – stories say – in honour of a namesake ancestor, Sir Edward Dering, who gave his Roundhead pursuers the slip during the Civil War by leaping to freedom through such a round-headed window.

Leave the churchyard by the south-west corner and turn right along the road to a T-junction by the Black Horse pub (926454). Cross the road and climb steps; keep ahead along a narrow path to turn right along a track (924456) to a road. Turn left here for 400 yards (400m). Opposite a lane with a 'cul-de-sac' sign turn right (922460), following a path over a field to the corner of a hedge. Continue over the next field to cross the stile halfway down the far hedge (929462). Cross the next field to a post with a yellow-tape top; then keep forward through a gate and down a lane between the houses of Jennings Farm to a road (932461). Turn left along the road for an unpleasant ¾ mile (1.2km) – there is a reasonable verge for at least some of the way, but please take care.

St Mary's Church ruin

At OS grid reference 934467 you'll pass the ruins of St Mary's Church on your right. The shattered tower retains most of its grandeur and grace; the body of the medieval building is a broken shell, with weeds smothering the floral tiles in the chancel floor. Gravestones lie around at all angles. An eerie place, whose clock of life stopped when a doodlebug or flying bomb struck it on 16 August 1944.

Beyond St Mary's the road crosses a river. In 100 yards (100m) turn left over a stile (936469) and follow a well-marked track to the left corner of a house and garden, then on to turn left along Hunger Hatch Lane (937476). At a T-junction (933479) turn right to cross the M20 and the railway cutting beyond. At the following T-junction turn right (934481); in 30 yards (30m) turn right again (FP fingerpost) over a stile and along a gravel road. In 50 yards (50m) turn left over a stile (FP fingerpost).

The route of the footpath for the next ¼ mile (0.4km) was not settled at the time of writing, owing to the ongoing building of the Channel Tunnel Rail Link. OS Explorer 137 shows horse paddocks at Newlands Stud which no longer exist. The best choice is to aim diagonally across the field to the bottom left corner beside some sheds, climb over the fence and turn left with the hedge on your left to reach a gate with a stile (937481). From here, aim half right across the corner of the field to go through a gap in the fence, and keep the same line to cross a stile. A yellow arrow shows the direction from here, cutting diagonally left across the corner of a rough field. This necessitates crossing two deep ditches which lack footplanks; so a better bet is to turn left after crossing the stile and work round the edge of the field (a brambly 50 yards/50m) before crossing a stile on your left into a green lane where you turn right.

In 100 yards (100m), at the end of the lane (940482), aim diagonally left across the field to cross a stile. Keep the same line across the next two fields; then keep ahead with a hedge on your right to cross the next stile and dogleg right and left round a pumping station (945485). Cross a stile and aim diagonally right to cross a stile in the hedge and turn left along the pavement for ½ mile (0.75km) to Charing Station.

PADDOCK WOOD, HOP FARM COUNTRY PARK, RIVER MEDWAY & CAPEL

This walk through the low-lying countryside of west Kent is full of associations with great Kentish hop harvests of the past. The 1000-acre (400-ha) hop farm at Beltring boasted the largest group of oast houses in Kent, and hosted several thousand East End hop pickers each autumn. Times have moved on – the Hop Farm Country Park has been established around the disused oasts, and you can relive the whole extraordinary story here. Further along the walk is a beautiful stretch of the River Medway, while down in the hamlet of Capel you can admire the church's 700-year-old wall-paintings. Hop gardens and fruit orchards abound, and the flatness of the terrain gives good far views under big, often dramatic skies.

Start & Finish:	Paddock Wood Station
Length of walk:	9 miles (15km)
OS maps:	1:50,000 Landranger 188, 1:25,000 Explorer 136
Travel:	By rail from London Charing Cross or London Waterloo East (50–55 mins); by road – M25 (Jct 5), A21 to Tonbridge, A26, B2017.
Features:	Hop Farm Country Park, Beltring; River Medway; medieval wall-paintings in the Church of St Thomas à Becket, Capel (see Further Information, pages 192–201, for details on obtaining the key).
Refreshments:	Hop Pocket Inn, Paddock Wood; King's Head PH, Five Oak Green; Dovecote Inn, Capel.

THE WALK

At Paddock Wood Station (671453) go through the gate in the station fence and bear left to meet the B2160 at the Hop Pocket Inn. Turn right along the pavement for 250 yards (250m); at a right bend turn left (670458) along a track towards a house with twin oasts. Pass the house, and in 70 yards

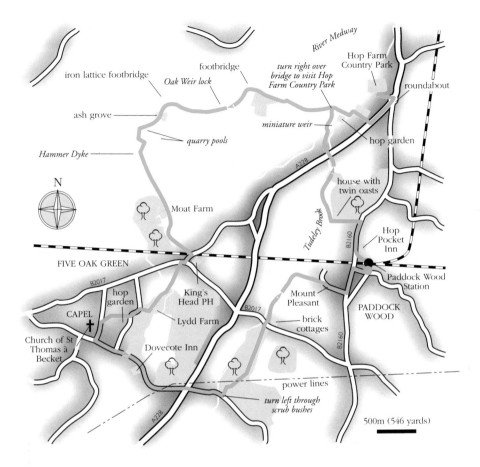

(70m) turn right (666458 – post with yellow arrow on left of track) along the field edge, with Tudeley Brook on your left, for ½ mile (0.75km) to the A228 (666465). Cross (take care!) and continue ('Public Footpath, River Medway 1m' fingerpost) up the left bank of Tudeley Brook. At the end of the first field go through the hedge and continue beside the brook. Pass a miniature two-step weir with a dark brick culvert, and in 200 yards (200m) reach a brick bridge across the brook (667471).

If you want to continue the walk without visiting the Hop Farm Country Park, see below. If you wish to visit the Hop Farm Country Park, turn right over the bridge and on along the left side of a hop garden. At the end, dogleg left and right, passing two houses to reach the A228 (671469). Turn left along the verge for 300 yards (300m) to a roundabout, and bear left to the entrance of the Hop Farm Country Park (673472).

Hop Farm Country Park

'Air and hops are wonderful restoratives. After passing an afternoon with the drier in the kiln, seated close to a great heap of hops and inhaling the odour, I was in a condition of agreeable excitement all the evening. My mind was full of fancy, imagination, flowing with ideas; a sense of lightness and joyousness lifted me up. I wanted music, and felt full of laughter. Like the half-fabled haschish, the golden bloom of the hops had entered the nervous system; intoxication without wine, without injurious after-effect, dream intoxication; they were wine for the nerves. If hops only grew in the Far East we should think wonders of so powerful a plant.'

The 19th-century writer Richard Jefferies catches the aura of fable and magic surrounding the sticky little bud that makes beer so deliciously bitter. The flat, damp claylands of this part of Kent are ideal for hop-growing. In the 1870s, 36,000 pickers from the East End of London would travel down each September to Kent for the hop harvest. Four thousand pickers were needed to supply the 20 oasts at the Whitbread brewery's Beltring hop farm.

Whitbread no longer grow their own hops at Beltring; cheaper, stronger hops from abroad have squashed the Kentish industry. Home-grown hops can be picked by machines these days, so the mass picking exoduses from London – half work, half holiday – are long gone. The Beltring farm is now a tourist attraction. In the splendid group of oasts with their conical caps, exhibitions have been mounted to tell the story through contemporary photographs, taped sound effects and stories. The squalor of the pickers' accommodation in Victorian times, philanthropic attempts to improve their living conditions, the hard work, banter, rough fun and games, all come to life. The Hop Farm Country Park also provides friendly giants of brewery horses to pat, and rough-and-tumble play areas for children. Outside is a small hop garden with poles, wires and strings, where you can pay to harvest your very own hops in September.

From the Hop Farm Country Park, return to the bridge over Tudeley Brook (667471) and keep forward along a field track. (If you have not visited the Hop Farm, turn left onto this field track opposite the Tudeley Brook bridge.) The track runs west through woodland, and on for ½ mile (0.75km) to reach the River Medway. Turn left here (661472 – Medway Valley Walk/MVW yellow arrow) along the south bank of the river.

Opposite: The white-cowled caps of oast towers overlook the buildings at the Hop Farm Country Park. Here, the hops were 'cured' or dried on horsehair blankets over charcoal and sulphur fires, then packed in sacks called 'pockets.'

River Medway

The wide estuarine mouth of the Medway, lined with famous maritime towns and dockyards like Chatham and Rochester, is a long way geographically and in spirit from this tranquil stretch of rural river. Under its ash and willow trees the Medway looks beautiful, flowing with an almost imperceptible movement. The river was canalised before the railway age to allow barge traffic to travel inland, and hereabouts is broken into sections separated by locks – hence the appearance of canal-like stillness.

Keep beside the river. In ¼ mile (0.4km) you pass a footbridge (657474) and join a track that reaches Oak Weir lock. Bear right off the track here to cross a footbridge (MVW yellow arrow); walk beside the lock, and keep on along the bank path for another ½ mile (0.75km) to reach an iron lattice footbridge (647473). Bear left here away from the river ('Five Oak Green 1½ m' fingerpost), with a hedge on your right. At the bottom of the field keep ahead through an ash grove on your right to cross a stile (645470). Yellow arrows direct you to the right, following a fence that skirts old quarry pools. At the far side of the field cross a footbridge and aim for a thin 4-foot (1.2-m) metal pole seen ahead across the field. Cross Hammer Dyke here by a concrete footbridge (643467).

On the far side two paths diverge; follow the left-hand one to cross a stile and bear right along a field edge. Follow the field edge as it bends left, and in 20 yards (20m) turn right over a concrete footbridge and walk along a track aiming for the three oasts of Moat Farm. At the edge of the farm (646461) bear left, then right along the left side of a big cold store. Cross a concrete road and bear right to follow a field edge up the right side of an orchard. Join the farm drive and follow it up to a road (649455). Turn right to reach the village green in Five Oak Green.

Turn left along the B2017 if you want to visit the King's Head PH; otherwise, turn right for 30 yards (30m), then left through an archway between Ivy House and Rose Cottage, and on along a fenced path. In 300 yards (300m) cross a watercourse and go over a stile (647450). In another 100 yards (100m) the path divides, take the right fork. In 50 yards (50m) cross a stile and bear left to reach the eccentric-looking oast at Lydd Farm (645448).

Lydd Farm

The two buildings nearest the track – the Clock House and the oast – make a strange but pleasing ensemble. The Clock House has a clock in a little dormer gable, curiously rounded corners, an ornate balcony and a cylindrical wooden side tower crowned by a bell turret. The cone of the oast is topped by a construction that looks like Dorothy Gale's flying house from *The Wizard of Oz*. In fact, it's an ingenious contraption fixed to the oast top by the farmer for practical purposes – opening the end doors of the device increases the draught to the fire below and makes the drying furnace hotter.

Cross the stile by Lydd Farm and turn right to the road. Bear left for 175 yards (175m), then right (642447 – FP fingerpost) along the right side of a hop garden. At the end, bear half-left to cross rough ground into a lane (638447). Turn left to reach the church in Capel (637445).

Church of St Thomas à Becket, Capel

Walking up the churchyard path you pass an ancient hollow yew almost 26 feet (7.9m) in girth; St Thomas à Becket is said to have preached beneath it in the 12th century, and it could easily date twice as far back.

Inside the Norman church you will find an extremely sturdy timber roof and, along the north wall, remarkable wall-paintings dating from about 1230–50. The wall paintings are in two tiers: the upper one is mostly vanished, while the lower one shows various, more or less decipherable, scenes. People look down from casements and hang bright cloths out of windows to welcome Christ's Entry into Jerusalem. In the splay of a window Cain bludgeons Abel to death, and is then ticked off by God. There is a fragmentary Last Supper, a half-obscured Betrayal and Christ appearing to Mary Magdalene on Easter Sunday.

At the T-junction below the chapel, turn left along the road for a not-very-pleasant ²/₃ mile (1km), passing the Dovecote Inn (643441) to reach the A228 (649438). Cross the road carefully and go down Crittenden Road ('Matfield' sign). In 250 yards (250m) cross a stream on a right bend; in another 50 yards (50m), just before a house on the left, turn left (653437 – concrete FP marker in the road verge) on a boggy path through scrub bushes. Keep the edge of the trees close on your right, and in 150 yards (150m) bear right through the fringe of the wood to keep ahead along the edge of an orchard with the wood now on your left. Go under power lines (654439), and in 50 yards (50m) leave the orchard through a gap in the hedge ahead. Aim diagonally right for the bottom right corner of the field, cross through a bramble hedge (stile with yellow arrows) and keep ahead up the right side of a long orchard to reach the B2017 (658446).

Cross the road and go up a stony track on the left side of a pair of brick cottages, continuing with a hedge and Tudeley Brook on your left. In ¹/₃ mile (0.5km) pass through a hedge; in another 150 yards (150m) turn right (662452) along a hedge-bank towards the houses of Paddock Wood. Cross a footbridge and walk along a fenced path between houses, then on along Mount Pleasant to reach the B2160 (668449), where you turn left. In 200 yards (200m), where the road begins to rise to cross the railway, turn right down steps ('Station' sign) to reach Paddock Wood Station.

HEVER & CHIDDINGSTONE

Two castles dominate this walk through the woods and clay farmlands of the Kentish Weald: Hever Castle, where the ill-fated Anne Boleyn spent her childhood and where she was later wooed by King Henry VIII; and Chiddingstone Castle, a Tudor house comprehensively turreted and castellated in fine romantic Gothic style in the early 19th century. Chiddingstone village is a tiny Tudor and Jacobean gem, with its ancient (and maybe druidical) Chiding Stone tucked away in the trees behind the main street. Woodland paths connect these varied delights, leading you through some of west Kent's loveliest countryside.

Start:	Hever Station
Finish:	Cowden Station
Length of walk:	7 miles (11km)
OS maps:	1:50,000 Landranger 188; 1:25,000 Explorer 147
Travel:	By rail from London Victoria (55 mins); by road – M25 (Jct 5 or 6), A25 to Westerham, B2026 to Edenbridge, minor road to Hever.
Features:	Hever Castle; St Peter's Church, Hever; oast houses and oak woods of the Kentish Weald; Chiddingstone Castle; St Mary's Church, village houses and Chiding Stone at Chiddingstone.
Refreshments:	King Henry VIII Inn, Hever; Hever Castle restaurant and tea-room; Castle Inn, Chiddingstone; Rock Inn, Hoath Corner.

THE WALK

From Hever Station (465445) walk up the station approach to turn right along the road. In 50 yards (50m) turn left over a stile (yellow arrow)

Opposite: It's a romantic, moated aspect for Hever Castle, and there is a most romantic story entwined throughout its walls – that of the passionate but ill-fated love affair between King Henry VIII and Anne Boleyn.

along a fenced path. In 300 yards (300m) cross a stile; the hedge on your right bears away to the right, but aim a little left of it over the field to cross a stile in the bottom hedge and bear left along a muddy green lane (471447) to a road. Turn right, and in 50 yards (50m) left (brown 'Hever Castle' sign). The road rounds a right bend; just after this, turn left over a stile (474448 – FP fingerpost and concrete footpath marker). In 100 yards (100m) turn right through a gate (yellow arrow) and across the corner of a field to cross a stile. Keep the hedge on your left for 100 yards (100m), then cross through it and walk up the right side of the hedge to cross a stile into the road. Turn right for 100 yards (100m) to find the gatehouse of Hever Castle on your left (476449).

Henry VIII and Anne Boleyn at Hever Castle

Hever Castle is one of England's most romantic castles, partly for its moat-girt position, cradled in a beautiful wooded valley, but chiefly because of the extraordinary and poignant love story that was played out within its walls. The famous tale of the love affair, marriage and deadly quarrel between King Henry VIII and Anne Boleyn never fails in its romantic appeal. It was here that Anne spent much of her early childhood, and here that Henry came as an ardent lover to court and win the beautiful 'Greensleeves' as his queen. The ghost of poor witchy Anne still haunts the castle.

Hever Castle was begun in 1270 as a fortified gatehouse and walled bailey inside a moat. In the late 15th century Sir Geoffry Bullen, a Norfolk man made good, bought the castle. It was his grandson Sir Thomas Bullen (or Boleyn), Anne's father, who built a Tudor house within the walls; its half-timbered walls and mellow brickwork survive there. Anne was born around 1501, perhaps at Hever (or maybe in 1504 at Rochford Hall in Essex, see page 83), and was just 12 when her ambitious father sent her to attend Queen Margaret of Austria at Brussels. Soon afterwards, Anne went to learn her manners and gain a sheen of sophistication at the French court, where she stayed until she was about 21. When she came back to England, groomed and polished, it was not long before King Henry's eye fell on her. Henry was married to Catherine of Aragon, but Catherine had failed to provide him with a male heir. The most extraordinary convulsions in English political and religious life ensued. Henry, in his passion for Anne and his furious disappointment with Catherine, would have his way, no matter what. So he initiated a permanent split with the Church of Rome, swept away the monasteries, and set up a new church with himself at its head. He married his Kentish love in January 1533; she was already pregnant with the future Queen Elizabeth I.

The portraits of Anne that hang at Hever Castle present her as attractive, elliptical of glance, potentially beguiling, but not of a beauty as devastating as one might expect, given her effect on the king. But all her charms and wiles availed Anne nothing when she failed to produce the male heir Henry needed. Three years after their marriage he was looking round again, with his eye on Jane Seymour. Anne was clapped into the Tower of London on trumped-up charges of adultery and incest, and was beheaded on Tower Green on 19 May 1536.

When Sir Thomas Bullen died in 1538, Hever Castle was claimed by King Henry VIII as a forfeit. It was one of the royal homes given by the king to his fourth wife, the 'Flanders mare' Anne of Cleves, as a sweetener when they were divorced after only six months of marriage.

Tour of the castle

A tour of the castle unfolds the story of Henry and Anne, the star-crossed lovers, and also tells the saga of the building's restoration in the early 20th century by William Waldorf Astor, the American multi-millionaire. Meticulous care was taken; for example, local craftsmen recreating 'Tudor' plaster ceilings were ordered to use the authentic materials that would have been employed by Tudor plaster workers, and to do their work 'by eye' alone, using no straight-edge measurement tools. Heavy Edwardian woodcarving lends weight and dignity to the various rooms, and a superb collection of 16th-century portraits of the key players in the 'Henry and Anne' drama brings history vividly to life. Perhaps the most poignant item on display in the castle is the 15th-century Book of Hours, gloriously handwritten and painted in Bruges around 1450, which belonged to Anne Boleyn. On the opening page of the penitential psalms appears, in Anne's faded handwriting, the inscription 'Le Temps Viendra, je Anne Boleyn' – 'My Time Will Come'.

Outside are beautiful gardens, formed from boggy meadows at the behest of William Waldorf Astor. They include a formal Italian garden, a fine geometric hedged maze, a curious bushy 'water maze' and a walk along the shore of the 35-acre (14-ha) lake which took Astor's workmen four years to dig and fill.

In St Peter's Church, just outside the castle gate, you will find the tomb and brass of Sir Thomas Bullen, Anne's father. Follow the path through the graveyard and then through trees ('Eden Valley Walk'/EVW arrows); it soon becomes a fenced path, shadowed by a private lane. Between the trees to your left there are glimpses of fine parkland and a gleam from the big lake. The path runs through the woods; then, ¾ mile (1.2km) after leaving Hever, it passes through a gate by a house (488448). Bear half right along the front of No. 2, Bothy Cottage, on a fenced path that crosses a road (491447 – FP fingerpost). Keep ahead along a muddy fenced path, along wood edges, and over scrubland of coppiced chestnut (there are several EVW waymarks). Descend through a little rock cutting and continue forward between cottages. At the road, turn left (498447) to reach the gate of Chiddingstone Castle (497453) on your right in ½ mile (0.75km).

Chiddingstone Castle

It was the Streatfeild family, local ironmasters grown rich through Wealden iron production, who built the core mansion of Chiddingstone around 1500. Three hundred years later Henry Streatfeild provided the house with crenellations, octagonal towers and turrets to turn it into a proper Gothic-style castle. The early 20th century saw a steep slide in the castle's fortunes, the nadir being reached after years of neglect and abuse while it was requisitioned during World War II. Then, in 1955, the art connoisseur and romantic Denys Bower bought Chiddingstone Castle and filled it with his eclectic collections of pictures, Buddhist temple art, Jacobite relics, Japanese porcelain and lacquer and Egyptian antiquities. The tour of the house shows off these extremely diverse treasures, collected by a man who was careless of his own comfort – he lived in the most ramshackle conditions in the castle, whose fabric he could not afford to repair – but who had an unerring eye for excellence.

Chiddingstone village

From the castle gate continue along the road. Turn right at the crossroads ('Chiddingstone' sign) to walk through Chiddingstone village. Chiddingstone, now in the care of the National Trust, is a wholly charming short strip of 16th- and 17th-century houses. The exterior walls of the Castle Inn are hung with dusky red earthenware tiles, its windows are diamond-panelled, its floors tiled.

Along the street, the 15th-century Burghesh Court used to be Chiddingstone's manor house; Anne Boleyn's father bought it in 1517. Now it houses a shop and tea-room. Opposite the shop stands St Mary's Church, whose parishioners have worked the church kneelers with local themes: the castle, oast houses, the rectory, Kentish flora and fauna and Zippy, the church cat.

The Chiding Stone

From the church continue along the village street to pass the school. Turn right here through a gate ('footpath to Chiding Stone' fingerpost) to follow a path to the Chiding Stone (501451). This handsome sandstone outcrop (not the first one you come to – the real stone is 10 yards/10m beyond) is shaped like a cottage loaf and stands some 13 feet (4m) high. It is an obvious, natural gathering place, and has been suggested as a site for druidical ceremonies, and maybe sacrifices. Nagging village wives were said to have been brought here to be admonished publicly: hence its title of the Chiding Stone. But Chiddingstone probably got its name more mundanely, from the 'ing' (or settlement) of a Saxon farmer named Cedd.

From the Chiding Stone return to the road and turn right. In 20 yards (20m) go right (FP fingerpost) along a fenced path; pass the village playing field, cross a stile and continue. Cross an open field to walk down the left side of a copse for 50 yards (50m). Turn right over a stile (yellow arrow). On the far side the path forks; take the right fork through the trees, and in 20 yards (20m) pass between two ponds. Keep ahead towards some barns to cross a stile (EVW waymark) and pass Hill Hoath Farm. At Hill Hoath House (on your right) bear right down a gravelled track to reach a road opposite 'Withers'; bear left here down a private road between cottages to pass through a gate (EVW and blue arrows). In 30 yards (30m) turn left over a stile (497446) and ascend to cross the stile visible ahead (yellow arrow). Keep a fence on your left and follow yellow arrows on posts to cross a stile in the top right corner of the field (495442). Turn left along a fenced path (yellow arrow) into woods. In 100 yards (100m) join a muddy rutted track; keep ahead for 100 yards (100m), then turn left (493438 – yellow arrow on post) through trees, then on across open grassy ground to reach a yellow arrow on a post. In 100 yards (100m) bear left through trees (492434). Emerge, and keep a fence on your left to reach a road (495431). Turn left for 150 yards (150m) if you want to visit the Rock Inn at Hoath Corner; otherwise, turn right along the road for ½ mile (0.75km) to a T-junction (490428).

Go over the T-junction, through a gate (FP fingerpost) and along a lane. In 300 yards (300m) a footpath fingerpost points right; cross the field here to a kissing gate in the far bottom corner and continue along the top edge of Bilton's Gill wood. Fifty yards (50m) before the edge of the wood trends left (486422), the path forks. Take the right fork steeply down through the trees to cross a footbridge and climb to cross a stile and leave the trees. Keep the hedge on your left for 200 yards (200m), then keep a cattle trough on your left and aim up the gradual slope of a field to reach the skyline among the trees of a hedge. Cross a stile here (483419) and keep ahead to pass a house and cross another stile into a lane. Turn left to descend to a T-junction (482416). Turn right to the road; bear left here, downhill, and in 200 yards (200m) turn right ('Cowden Station' sign) to Cowden Station (476417).

DORMANSLAND, HAXTED MILL & LINGFIELD

This walk passes by green lanes and stony tracks through a particularly beautiful tract of east Surrey. During the walk you'll see Lingfield's famous race-course, the moated site of Starborough Castle, picturesque Haxted Mill with its restored wooden milling machinery, and one of Surrey's best collections of medieval tomb monuments in Lingfield parish church. There's a bonus too – there are no fewer than three places where you can stand with one foot in the eastern and one in the western hemisphere!

Start:	Dormans Station
Finish:	Lingfield Station
Length of walk:	9 miles (14km)
OS maps:	1:50,000 Landranger 187; 1:25,000 Explorer 146, 147
Travel:	By rail from London Victoria or London Bridge (50 mins approx.); by road – M25 (Jct 6), A22 south to Blindley Heath, B2029 to Lingfield, minor road to Dormans Station.
Features:	Lanes and woodlands of east Surrey; Starborough Castle moated site; Haxted Mill; Church of St Peter and St Paul, Lingfield.
Refreshments:	Plough Inn, Dormansland; Riverside Brasserie, Haxted Mill; Star Inn, Lingfield.

THE WALK

From the platform at Dormans Station (396415) climb the steps and turn left along the front of the station building, then immediately left (FP fingerpost) along a tarmac path over a common. In 300 yards (300m) the path reaches a crossroads (398416), where you turn left along Mill Lane.

Mill Lane and the Meridian

The crossroads on Mill Lane lies exactly on the Greenwich Meridian – 0° of longitude – so those with a leg stretch as wide as their imagination can bestraddle the seam of the world! Mill Lane is rough-surfaced, leaf-carpeted and sun-dappled; the kind of country lane that many people think died out with the advent of the motor car. Through gaps in the hedge you soon get views over the white-railed gallops of Lingfield Park Race Course, which has been hosting race meetings for well over 100 years.

Soon you cross the railway (397418), then a golf course, and continue into woods. In 200 yards (200m) turn right at a crossroads of tracks (396424 – '18th Tee' fingerpost). In 150 yards (150m), blue arrows on a post on the right of the track point you to the right on a gravel path which crosses the golf course (beware flying balls!) and runs beneath the railway (399426). At West Street keep ahead along a residential lane to cross a road (403427 – FP fingerpost). Continue along the path to another road, where you turn right for 200 yards (200m) to a crossroads (406428 – Plough Inn to the right). Cross over and keep ahead along Ford Manor Road. In 300 yards (300m) pass Ford House and take the right fork in the road ('Greathed Manor' sign and PB fingerpost).

Pass the entrances to Greathed Manor and Ford Manor (416425), keeping ahead ('Courtyard' sign) and following fingerposts with horseshoe logos. In 200 yards (200m) the path splits beside a pond. Take the left fork up the left side of a weatherboarded barn (418424); follow the track sharply to the left here, then round a right bend in front of buildings in red-and-black brick. The track continues into trees, then as a hedged path through the fields to pass Littleworth Cottage (424426). In 50 yards (50m) follow the lane as it bends left; in another 50 yards (50m) where the lane bends right, bear left through a gate (blue arrow and Vanguard Way/VW sign) along a green lane. Skirt a small wood, and keep ahead on the far side (horseshoe fingerpost) to a road (423434). Bear right for 20 yards (20m), then left over a stile (VW yellow arrow and FP fingerpost). Walk diagonally right across the field, aiming about two-thirds of the way up the opposite hedge to cross a stile (425437), and turn left along the driveway to Starborough Castle (426441).

Starborough Castle

Through the railings you catch a glimpse of trees, landscaped banks and flowerbeds, statues and water features – also of a Georgian battlemented

Opposite: The now peaceful scene at Haxted Mill, where the mill-stream water bubbles into the millpond under a pretty bridge, was a hive of industrious activity from Tudor times through to the mid-20th century.

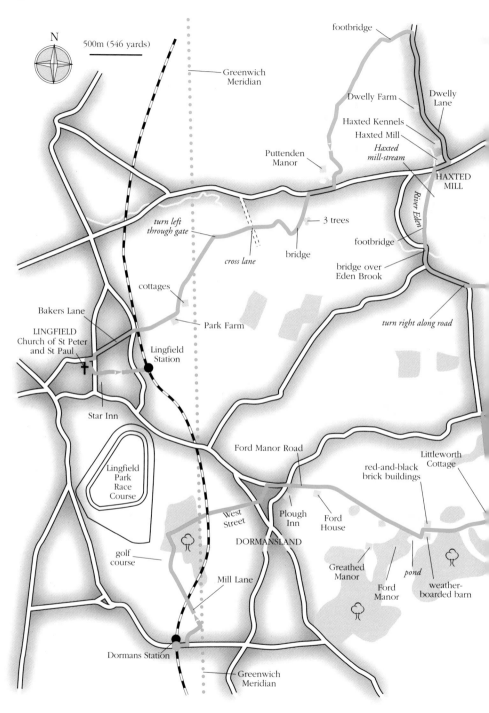

N

500m (546 yards)

Greenwich Meridian

footbridge

Dwelly Farm

Dwelly Lane

Haxted Kennels

Haxted Mill

Haxted mill-stream

Puttenden Manor

HAXTED MILL

River Eden

turn left through gate

3 trees

bridge

footbridge

cross lane

bridge over Eden Brook

cottages

turn right along road

Bakers Lane

Park Farm

LINGFIELD Church of St Peter and St Paul

Lingfield Station

Star Inn

Lingfield Park Race Course

Ford Manor Road

Littleworth Cottage

red-and-black brick buildings

West Street

Plough Inn

Ford House

golf course

DORMANSLAND

Greathed Manor

pond

weather-boarded barn

Mill Lane

Ford Manor

Dormans Station

Greenwich Meridian

136

Cernes Farm

bear left up farm drive

Starborough
Castle

Hoopers Farm

*50 yards (50m)
beyond left bend, bear
left through gate*

summerhouse and a fine, dignified, brick house. But Starborough Castle itself, built by the 1st Lord Cobham in the 1340s, has long vanished from its square moated site.

The Cobhams were one of the greatest families of medieval England, friends and confidants of royalty. The 3rd Lord Cobham fought at the Battle of Agincourt in 1415 and, as a mark of respect, was granted the custodianship of the captured Duc d'Orléans, father of King Louis XII. He brought the duc back with him to Starborough, the first of many country residences where the unfortunate man was to languish in feather-bedded captivity for the following 20 years. The Cobhams championed kings of England in the lists and fought for them on many battlefields.

Starborough Castle is strictly private property. Beside its gates turn left over a stile (VW yellow arrow), then right along the field edge with the hedge on your right. On the far side of the property cross a stile and turn right along a lane for 50 yards (50m), then bear left (425442) up a farm drive (NB the VW yellow arrow is badly placed here, implying that you cross a stile on your left – don't!). In 100 yards (100m) you pass a post with two yellow arrows. One points right; follow the other VW arrow ahead towards Cernes Farm for 70 yards (70m), then turn left over a stile (426445). Follow the direction shown by the VW yellow arrow. Cross a footbridge and a stile, and keep ahead to the top left corner of the next field where you cross a stile into a road (421445) and turn right (VW sign). In 400 yards (400m) pass a single-track road on your left, and in another 50 yards (50m) cross a bridge over the Eden Brook. On the far side turn right over a stile (418447 – FP fingerpost) and go over the field to cross the River Eden by a footbridge (417450). Keep ahead between the river and Haxted mill-stream to reach the road at Haxted Mill (419455).

Haxted Mill

Haxted Mill is a beautiful old building, weatherboarded and white-painted under a roof of red tiles. Its eastern half was built in 1794, but the western portion dates back to Tudor times. A sack dangles by a chain outside. Inside the four-storey watermill the cogged wooden gear wheels are in good working order. There are old mill wheels, displays on milling through the ages and such recondite items as 'hoppers', 'shoes' and 'horses' – none of which is anything like it sounds! Beside the old mill, water flows into the millpond under an ornate little bridge. The Riverside Brasserie alongside is a good spot for lunch, on the terrace beside the pool.

Leaving the mill, turn left (east) along the road for 150 yards (150m), a nasty stretch in a narrow cutting; then turn left along Dwelly Lane ('Oxted' and 'Surrey Cycleway' signs) – also a motor road, but a quieter one. Pass Haxted Kennels and Dwelly Farm, then pass through a copse. As you leave the trees, turn left through a gate (466466). Follow the fence round to the left to cross a stile in the far left corner of the field (yellow arrow). Bear left to cross a brook by a footbridge; follow the yellow arrow direction across the field to pass through a gap in the far hedge just to the right of a clump of trees. Keep the hedge on your right and follow the field edge. At the end of this field, go through a hedge gap (411462), and walk across the following diamond-shaped field, crossing a stile in the furthest corner. Cross the next field to the far right corner; cross the stile here (409457) and bear left along a wide path between hedges. At the bottom, follow yellow arrows to the left and round Puttenden Manor to the road (410453).

Turn right, pass one FP fingerpost on the left, and in 200 yards (200m) turn left over a stile (408453 – FP fingerpost and yellow arrow). Steer diagonally right across a field, aiming for three trees standing together a little to the left of telegraph poles. Cross Eden Brook by a bridge here (406450). On the far side bear right (yellow arrow) and follow the brook for 500 yards (500m) to go over a stile (yellow arrow) onto a lane (403450). Cross the lane and go through the gate opposite. Follow the direction of the yellow arrow to cross a ditch in a line of trees, then aim a little left across the next field towards a gate in the far hedge.

Just before you reach it, turn left through a gate in the left-hand hedge (399449). Keep forward with a hedge on your left and the spire of Lingfield church ahead and slightly to the right. At the bottom of the field go through a gate, over a stile (397445) and on along a green lane. Pass cottages on your left, then a FP fingerpost on your right. Keep ahead, and in 15 yards (15m) bear right along the front of Park Farm farmhouse (396442). Pass the gates of the farmhouse and continue along the gravelled lane to cross the railway on the level (393441) into the eastern outskirts of Lingfield. Cross a road and go down Bakers Lane opposite; at the top of the road bear left along Church Road. In 10 yards (10m) a footpath on the right of the road leads through the churchyard to the Church of St Peter and St Paul (389438).

Church of St Peter and St Paul, Lingfield

The glory of this church is its richly carved and decorated tombs and its superb brasses to members of the Cobham family. The effigy of Reginald, the 1st Lord Cobham, lies on the south side of the Lady chapel. His head rests on a Saracen-head helm and his feet on another Saracen, a little figure dressed in a red robe and black slippers, with a comical air of frowning resignation as he shoulders Lord Cobham's enormous pointed iron shoes. The knight was the builder of Starborough Castle, and fought both at Crécy (1346) and Poitiers (1356).

Against the north wall of the Lady chapel is the dark marble tomb of the 2nd Lord Cobham, inlaid with a wonderful elaborate brass. 'Brave as a leopard,' runs his inscription, 'lavish in his housekeeping; handsome, genial, munificent and generous.' Brasses featuring Cobham ladies in beautiful dresses fill the chapel floor between the two knights, father and son.

In front of the high altar is the most sumptuous tomb of all, topped by the alabaster effigies of the 3rd Lord Cobham and his wife Ann Bardolf, their feet resting on a pair of curious little dragons. This Lord Cobham was one of Henry V's 'band of brothers' who fought beside him at the Battle of Agincourt in 1415. In 1431 he founded a college in Lingfield, and had the church magnificently rebuilt. It seemed one more high point in a family story of perpetual success; but within 25 years the Cobhams were extinct.

The 3rd Lord Cobham's lovely and spirited daughter Eleanor married Humphrey, Duke of Gloucester. According to William Shakespeare's *Henry VI*, Eleanor provoked a surge of jealousy in the king's wife. Eleanor was arraigned on trumped-up charges of treason and sorcery, and condemned to lifelong incarceration in the Isle of Man.

Leave the churchyard by the south-east corner, passing Church Gate Cottage to cross a road (389437). Walk down the left side of the Star Inn along a tarmac footpath that crosses open ground to reach a road (393437); cross the road to reach Lingfield Station.

BALCOMBE, ARDINGLY RESERVOIR & WAKEHURST PLACE

Woodlands and water dominate this lovely walk through the Wealden landscape of North Sussex. Ardingly Reservoir gives a fine waterside walk with plenty of opportunity for bird-watching, while the oak, pine and beech woods that clothe the slopes and hilltops are beautiful to walk through. There's a great story attached to the Culpeper brasses in St Peter's Church at Ardingly (pronounced 'Arding–*lie*'). The Culpeper family lived at nearby Wakehurst Place for centuries; the estate now forms a rural outstation of the Royal Botanic Gardens at Kew, where you can enjoy rare plants and trees and explore the delights of the Millennium Seed Bank.

Start & Finish:	Balcombe Station
Length of walk:	9 miles (14km)
OS maps:	1:50,000 Landranger 187, 1:25,000 Explorer 135
Travel:	By rail from London Bridge (40 mins) or London Victoria (50 mins); by road – M25 (Jct 7/8), M23 (Jct 10a), B2036.
Features:	Ardingly Reservoir (bring binoculars for bird-watching); Culpeper and Wakehurst brasses in St Peter's Church, Ardingly; Wakehurst Place Royal Botanic Gardens and Tudor mansion and Millennium Seed Bank; woodlands of the Sussex Weald.
Refreshments:	Balcombe Tea Rooms and Half Moon PH, Balcombe; Wakehurst Place Restaurant.

THE WALK

From Balcombe Station (307301) climb steps and cross the B2036 by a telephone box. Climb the path and bear right along residential Oldlands Avenue for ½ mile (0.75km) to a T-junction (315302). Turn left, and in 150

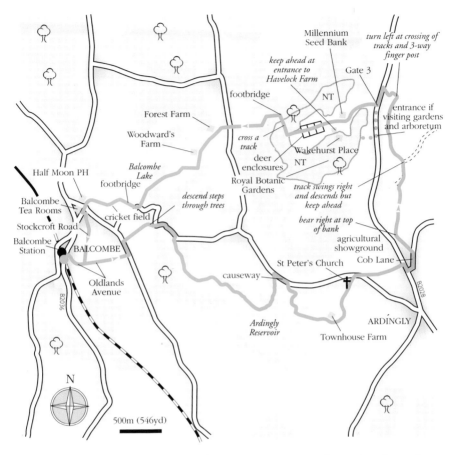

yards (150m) go right across a stile (concrete PB marker). Go through a gate, and follow the path over a field and down by the right side of a wood. At the bottom corner of the wood pass a large gate and PB fingerpost on your left, and in 10 yards (10m) turn left through a kissing gate and descend steps through the trees to a road (318305). Turn right to cross the 'wrist' of Ardingly Reservoir's western arm. Follow the road uphill for 200 yards (200m), then turn right through a gate (319304 – PB fingerpost and Ardingly Reservoir notice). Descend to the water's edge and bear left along the margin of the reservoir.

Ardingly Reservoir

The V-shaped system of valleys between Balcombe and Ardingly was flooded in 1977 to create this big artificial lake. Ardingly is a particularly beautiful reservoir with a curving shoreline, reed and wetland areas, and thickly wooded banks. The trees are mainly larch, pine and silver birch, with patches of older hazel coppice and sweet chestnut. By the water grow small oaks and willows. Warblers and other songbirds thrive in the woods, while the big sheet of water is a natural magnet for water-birds – coots, moorhens, great crested grebes and other divers, along with Canada geese in big flocks and cormorants and herons fishing the shallows. Bird-watching hides stand out in the water on stalky legs – so don't forget your binoculars!

Follow the shore path for 1⅓ miles (2km) to reach a road (331299), where you turn right to cross the eastern arm of the reservoir by a causeway. On the far side turn right through a kissing gate (FP fingerpost) and continue along the waterside footpath. On the far side of the second bay turn left over a stile (333295 – FP fingerpost) and climb the slope to cross another stile (FP fingerpost). Walk up the field with a hedge on your left. At the top, cross a stile and continue along a lane (at first deeply rutted) which leads past Townhouse Farm (338293) before curving left to run up through houses to St Peter's Church at Ardingly (340298).

The Culpeper abductions

St Peter's is a 14th-century church of grey and yellow stone with a squat, sturdy tower and a timber porch. Beneath an ornate tabernacle against the north wall of the sanctuary is an altar tomb which holds a fine brass to Sir Richard Wakehurst (died 1434) and his wife Elizabeth. Under the chancel aisle carpet are four more beautiful brasses, two of them commemorating brothers Nicholas and Richard Culpeper. 'Nichas' is shown in armour beside his wife Elizabeth, who wears a long head-dress and an elaborately embroidered girdle, while 'Ric' Culpeper lies by his wife Margarete.

The brothers did not gain their ladies through gentle courtship. Elizabeth and Margarete Wakehurst were heiresses to the Wakehurst lands and fortunes, and orphans – a nice catch for 'a pair of ruthless fortune hunters', as the Culpeper brothers have been labelled. On the death of their father, the girls were placed under the protection of Sir John Culpeper, elder brother to Nicholas and Richard; but that did not prevent the young men turning up fully armed to abduct the heiresses. Amid 'great and piteous lamentation and weeping', Elizabeth and Margarete were

Opposite: The handsome Tudor mansion of Wakehurst Place stands at the centre of wonderful gardens. These gardens are maintained by the Royal Botanic Gardens of Kew as an environment where many rare and delicate plant species can flourish in sheltered conditions.

forcibly removed and forthwith married to the brothers. As things turned out, Margarete died childless; but Nicholas and Elizabeth Culpeper produced 10 sons and eight daughters, whose stiff little images you can see etched into the brass below their parents.

At the T-junction by St Peter's, turn right along the road; then in 10 yards (10m) bear left (FP fingerpost) down a track. In 50 yards (50m) go through a gate and turn right on a tarmac (later concrete) track along the south edge of the South of England Agricultural Showground. At the B2028 (346300) turn right for 100 yards (100m); cross with care, and turn left down Cob Lane. In 300 yards (300m) bear left (347301 – PB fingerpost) up a woodland track. At the top of the bank bear right (345303 – PB fingerpost) through the woods, losing height gradually. In ½ mile (0.75km) a stony trackway comes in from the left; then in 100 yards (100m) a PB fingerpost points you on ahead. In another 20 yards (20m) the trackway swings right and descends steeply (346311), but keep ahead here.

In another ½ mile (0.75km) you reach a crossing of tracks (346319) at a three-way PB fingerpost, with a gateway marked 'Private, Keep Out' to your right. Turn left here along a track. In 50 yards (50m) the track divides, take the left fork (PB fingerpost). In another 50 yards (50m) branch to the right (PB fingerpost) on a narrow track which climbs to the B2028 (344320). Cross the road and turn left along the grass verge for 300 yards (300m) until you reach Gate 3 entrance to the grounds of Wakehurst Place. If you want to visit the gardens and arboretum, continue along the road verge for a little way to turn right across a car-park to the ticket kiosk and entrance.

Wakehurst Place

Sir Edward Culpeper built the mansion of Wakehurst Place in 1590, by which time the ancient Kent and Sussex family was already in decline from its medieval heyday. Later Culpepers got themselves into financial fixes – one even had to sell the entire estate for £9,000 to cover his gambling debts. In 1903, the amateur but expert botanist Sir Gerald Loder bought Wakehurst Place, and created 170 acres (70ha) of superb gardens over the following 30 years. In 1963, the house, gardens and woodlands – along with £200,000 – were given to the National Trust by the then owner, menswear millionaire Sir Henry Price of 'Fifty Shilling Tailors' fame. The National Trust leases the property to the Royal Botanic Gardens at Kew, which runs it as an outstation.

The dry, sandy soil of north Sussex succours species that might not do so well on the damp London clay of Kew – here the climate is milder, the air cleaner and the situation more sheltered. A collection of shrubs and trees of world importance has been built up at Wakehurst. The tree collection, one of the finest in Britain, features exotics from the Himalaya, North America, the Mediterranean and both the Near and Far East, as well as the native oaks, pines and beeches that have been retained. The plant collection has been planned to give spectacular shows throughout the year, from daffodil sheets in spring through cottage garden plants and orchids in summer to a winter garden full of scented and coloured plants and scrub trees. There's also a superb mosaic of habitat in the 150-acre (60-ha) Loder Valley Reserve, an area carefully managed for the benefit of badgers, deer, dormice and other animals, birds and insects native to the Sussex Weald.

Millennium Seed Bank

Outside the perimeter of the National Trust property is the Millennium Seed Bank, housed in barrel-roofed glasshouses that look like ultra-modern versions of Victorian train sheds. This is an exciting international project to collect, freeze and preserve the seed of up to 24,000 plant species from all over the world. You can stroll around the cases displaying seeds with the appearance of abstract sculpture, seeds huge and tiny, fossil seeds and seeds arranged like artistic installations. Behind glass screens the Seed Bank's scientists go about their work of preserving, germinating, propagating and cataloguing the seeds, seemingly indifferent to the fascinated onlookers.

If you are not visiting the arboretum and gardens, turn right off the B2028 through Gate 3, and follow the drive past the Millennium Seed Bank (340317). Follow the footpath (FP fingerpost) down the left side of the Seed Bank. At the entrance of Havelock Farm (338316) keep ahead on a gravelly track between fences. In 50 yards (50m) pass through a kissing gate (FP fingerpost) and continue along a path between deer-fences and through deer-gates, to cross a stile into the woods (333315).

Woods around Wakehurst

These woods form the southern remnants of the Forest of Worth, which, together with St Leonard's Forest, draped a vast blanket of trees across the High Weald of Sussex in medieval times. In the Tudor era, yeomen farmers were felling trees and cutting farms out of the heathland and wildwood, and by the 18th century the forest was greatly diminished. Nevertheless, there are still plenty of beautiful beeches, oaks, sweet chestnuts and ash trees, and a scatter of hammer ponds as a reminder of the medieval ironworking industry that enriched local ironmasters and polluted the countryside.

As you enter the woods head downhill, following the FP fingerpost. In 100 yards (100m) cross a track at a two-finger FP fingerpost and keep ahead along the footpath, through a tall kissing gate and on down to cross a footbridge. In 50 yards (50m) turn left (332317 – FP fingerpost) to cross two more streams and climb to the edge of the wood. Go through a big wooden gate to leave the wood through a metal gate (331317). Turn left and follow the wood edge, bending right to continue for ¼ mile (0.4km) and cross a stile into a road (326315). Turn right for 10 yards (10m), then left along a stony lane ('Forest Farm' sign and FP fingerpost). In 150 yards (150m) the lane swings right towards Forest Farm; keep ahead here across a stile ('High Weald Circular Walk' red arrow and FP fingerpost) to continue with a hedge on your left. Cross a stile at the bottom of the field (323313) and bear diagonally left across the next field, following the FP fingerpost direction. Cross the stile on the far side (FP fingerpost) and turn right along the top of the next field to cross a stile and turn left along a farm lane (321311).

Follow the lane to cross the foot of Balcombe Lake and meet a road. In 40 yards (40m) turn right through a kissing gate (315307 – FP fingerpost) to descend a field and cross a footbridge. Follow the hedge up to the top left corner of the field, and bear left with a hedge on your right to go through a kissing gate (313308 – FP fingerpost) and along a track. Follow it across a cricket field and through a hedge gap into a lane (312307). Turn right to reach a crossroads in Balcombe (309307). Cross, and walk along Bramble Hill for 30 yards (30m); turn left opposite Balcombe Tea Rooms along Stockcroft Road for ⅓ mile (0.5km) to Oldlands Avenue (309301). Turn right here to return to Balcombe Station.

POLESDEN LACEY & RANMORE COMMON

Beautiful woods on the shoulders of the Surrey downs, sweeping views across two deep valleys, a great country house and a stretch of England's oldest road – these are some of the delights of this walk. It explores a much-favoured corner of the North Downs, preserved for the enjoyment of all by a curious mixture of private generosity and public farsightedness. At centre stage stands Polesden Lacey, a classic English country house, where the spirit of sharp-tongued Edwardian hostess Mrs Ronald Greville still rules the roost. A highlight of the house, now in the care of the National Trust, is its three-sided Picture Corridor hung with dozens of 17th-century Dutch landscapes and other Old Master paintings. Moving from this hothouse of social manners and artifice through the tangled wildwood of Ranmore Common to tread the ancient North Downs Way in the footsteps of Bronze Age traders offers a pleasingly steep set of contrasts.

Start & Finish: Boxhill and Westhumble Station
Length of walk: 9 miles (14km)
OS maps: 1:50,000 Landranger 187; 1:25,000 Explorer 146
Travel: By rail from London Victoria or London Waterloo (46 mins); by road – (M25 Jct 9), A24.
Features: Fanny Burney plaque at Westhumble; Norbury Park Estate; Polesden Lacey; Ranmore Common; North Downs Way; St Bartholomew's Church; Westhumble Chapel ruin.
Refreshments: Stepping Stones PH, Westhumble; Polesden Lacey tea-room.

THE WALK

Boxhill and Westhumble railway station (167518) – the starting point for this walk – is a fine example of the lengths that Victorian railway companies went to in order to impress and flatter their customers. The pillar capitals and corbels of the porch at the little halt on the

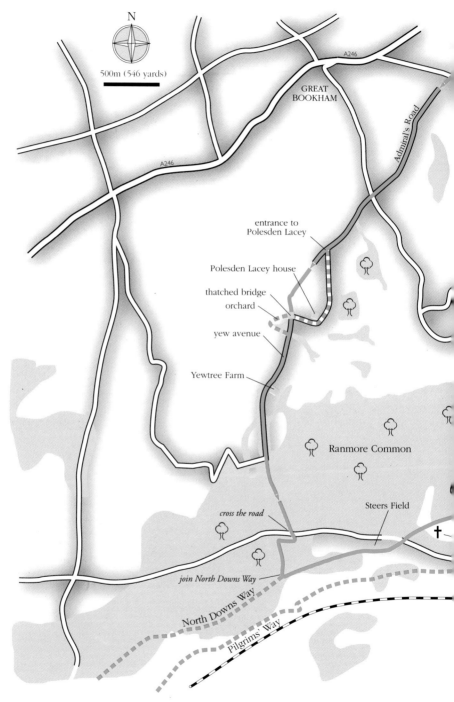

N

500m (546 yards)

A246

GREAT
BOOKHAM

A246

Admiral's Road

entrance to
Polesden Lacey

Polesden Lacey house

thatched bridge
orchard

yew avenue

Yewtree Farm

Ranmore Common

Steers Field

cross the road

join North Downs Way

North Downs Way

Pilgrims' Way

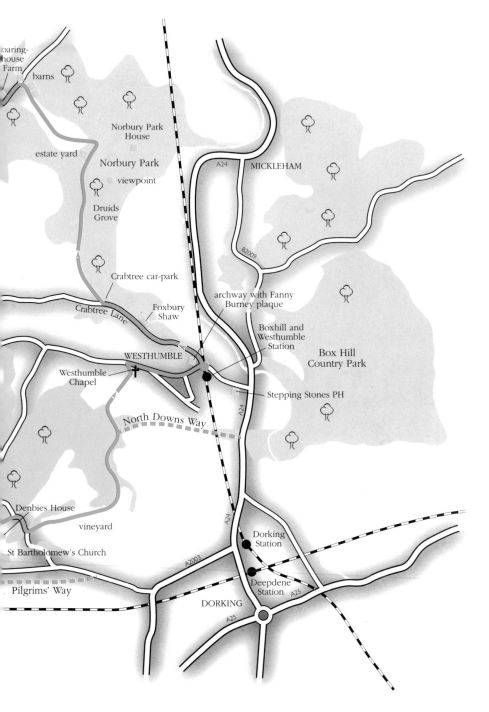

Leatherhead–Dorking line were furnished with fine carvings of fruit and flowers, which still enchant those who use the station.

Fanny Burney and Westhumble

Leaving the station, make for the large flint and stone archway ahead. Its blue plaque records the residence in Westhumble of celebrated Georgian novelist and diarist Fanny Burney and her husband, the French exile General d'Arblay. The bubbly Fanny had published her novel *Camilla* in 1796, and was in demand as a guest. She had made great friends with the Locke family of nearby Norbury Park, and it was they who gave her land at Westhumble on which to build 'Camilla Cottage'. On the day in 1797 that Fanny and her husband moved in, the impetuous General went 'striding over hedge and ditch' in his hurry to get to the new house – which was completely unfurnished, containing only 'a glorious fire of wood, and a little bench, borrowed of one of the carpenters: nothing else.' The couple were happy enough in Camilla Cottage, however, as they walked, socialised and gardened – the General once dug up an entire asparagus bed under the impression that it was a patch of weeds.

From the archway, bear right along Crabtree Lane, with views to your right of the white bulk of Norbury Park House on its sweep of green lawns in a clearing in the woods. Pass 'Foxbury' on your right, and in ¼ mile (0.4km) bear right through Crabtree car-park (158525 – PB). Continue along the western edge of the wood on a bridleway, which soon becomes a surfaced track.

Norbury Park Estate

Surrey County Council bought up the 1,300 acres (520ha) of the Norbury Park Estate in 1930, an act of farsightedness that saved this mosaic of farmland, chalk grassland and woodland from housing development. The bridleway you are following is just one of many that run through mixed woodland of beech, ash and cherry – trees highly characteristic of these flinty chalk downs – along with maple, sycamore and hazel coppice. Blackbirds, tits and warblers thrive in these woods, and you may hear the scutter of squirrels and the occasional crash of a roe deer breaking through the undergrowth. Primroses and bluebells do well under the trees and along the paths in spring, but none grows in the cold shade of Druids Grove (157533). Here you'll find ancient yews with iron-hard limbs, some of them perhaps 2,000 years old. Beyond the grove, a signposted viewpoint

Opposite: From the open flank of Box Hill there are sweeping views across the low-lying Wealden landscape, which is thickly wooded and patched by hedges into countless squares of brown and green.

just to the east of the bridleway gives superb views out from the trees across the valley of the River Mole to Juniper Hill. Away to the right stands the dark, tree-cloaked rise of Box Hill, the favourite 1950s and 1960s Bank Holiday destination of London's motorbikers.

A glance to your left here will show you the large conservatories and white, many-windowed walls of Norbury Park House (160537) close at hand. The house was built in 1774 for the Locke family, friends and benefactors of Fanny Burney. By then the estate had already been stripped of much of its woodland, its beautiful walnut trees having been sold to make musket stocks for the Army. In 1890, Norbury Park was bought by Leopold Salmon – he also bought Box Hill and presented it to the National Trust. The house's most famous 20th-century inhabitant was Dr Marie Stopes, brave and controversial pioneer of family planning clinics, who lived here until her death in 1957.

Back on the track, continue north to pass the estate yard on your left. Just beyond, bear left at a picnic place (158538) to follow a good stony bridleway out of the trees. It curves right-handed between woods, then in ½ mile (0.75km) bends left by some barns (152541). In 100 yards (100m) turn left at a four-way fingerpost ('Bookham'). Within 200 yards (200m) you reach the splendid old weatherboarded barn at Roaringhouse Farm (149541).

Turn right here up a track for 300 yards (300m) to the crest of the ridge, then go left ('Public Byway' fingerpost) along a track called Admiral's Road, with fine roof-of-the-downs views all round. The new houses of Great Bookham, crowding almost up to Admiral's Road, are a sharp reminder of how much walkers owe the previous generations who fought to maintain these downs in their green and wooded state.

In ⅓ mile (0.5km) keep ahead at a crossing of paths (148539) along a hedged lane to a road (141533). Keep ahead (brown 'Polesden Lacey' sign) on a footpath on the right side of the road for ⅓ mile (0.5km) to the arched entrance to Polesden Lacey on the left (137527). NB If not visiting Polesden Lacey, keep ahead here, bearing left in 200 yards (200m) along the west side of the property to rejoin the route at the top of a yew avenue (133521).

Polesden Lacey

For a country house with such a grand reputation Polesden Lacey (136522) stands surprisingly low, a two-storey building in cheerful yellow and white, its two wings running forward to end in pretty bow fronts. A central clock tower rises in the middle of the ensemble. 'Polesdene' appears in written records going back nearly 700 years, but the current house dates to an 1824 rebuild of the Polesden Lacey that a former owner, dramatist Richard Brinsley Sheridan, thought 'the nicest place, within a prudent distance of London, in England.' Sheridan bought the estate in 1797, the year that Fanny Burney moved into Camilla Cottage just down the road. He made a terraced walk, set up a good library and installed his beloved second wife. 'It shall be,' he promised, 'a seat of health and happiness where she shall chirp like a bird, bound like a fawn and grow fat as a little pig.'

The Hon. Mrs Ronald Greville certainly chirped like a bird when she was in residence in the early 20th century, shooting her famed and feared poison darts of malicious wit among the kings and queens, dukes and duchesses who filled her drawing room and gathered round her extremely well-appointed dining table. And, by all accounts, it was Mrs Greville's butler Bacon who grew fat as a little pig on a steady clandestine intake of his employer's delicacies and fine wines. Mrs Greville loved a lord, and a monarch even more. King Edward VII came to stay, Queen Mary was a friend, and as for the Duke and Duchess of York (later King George VI and Queen Elizabeth) – Mrs Greville appointed herself a kind of honorary favourite aunt to the young couple, who honeymooned at Polesden Lacey in 1923. The mettlesome hostess ('Maggie Greville! I would sooner have an open sewer in my drawing room!' – Lady Leslie) filled Polesden Lacey with fine pictures, porcelain, furniture and silver.

Truth to tell, Maggie Greville was no better than she ought to have been. She was the illegitimate daughter of a rich Scottish brewer and his lover, the wife of the brewery's day porter. Maggie used to say, 'I'd rather be a beeress than an heiress,' but she grew up to court and respect money, power and position. In the 1930s, along with several of her contemporaries, she became an admirer of Nazism. She had an acid tongue, and could be a formidable enemy. But she was also generous and warm-hearted, one of life's radiators. When she died in 1942 she left Polesden Lacey to the National Trust with the wish that it should always be open to the public – not the sentiments of an unregenerate snob, as she is sometimes painted.

In the Picture Corridor at Polesden Lacey there is a telling portrait of Mrs Greville painted in 1891 at the time of her marriage – a vivacious, humorous-looking young beauty with sparkling black eyes, warm in her fur cloak. Take your time strolling around the corridor – many wonderful paintings are hung on the dark panelled walls. Notable are the 17th-century Dutch canal scenes and seascapes such as Aert van der Neer's wintry skaters in *A Town on a Frozen River*, the coastal landscape and inshore shipping in *The Zuider Zee Coast near Muiden* by Jacob van Ruisdael, and a mournful bull beside a lake by bovine specialist Aelbert Cuyp. The Drawing Room is smothered in gold leaf and Green Men, beautiful hand-painted Meissen porcelain adorns the study, and in the Smoking Room there is a gaggle of royal photographs, including King Edward VII (his signature is the first in the Polesden Lacey visitors' book on display), the Prince of Thurm and Taxis, the Maharajah of Cooch Behar and Alice Keppel, Edward VII's ripe peach of a mistress.

There are 30 acres (12ha) of Edwardian gardens to explore before you make your departure from Polesden Lacey by way of the walled garden and a thatched bridge over a sunken lane to the west of the house. Go diagonally left from the bridge to the bottom left-hand corner of the orchard beyond (132522); at the gate turn sharp left along the wood edge. In 200 yards (200m) go through a gate to the top of the yew avenue (133521 – alternative route rejoins here). Do not take the surfaced lane ahead ('Polesden Farm' sign), but turn right downhill (blue arrow) on a raised causeway through the yew avenue. Keep to the right of Yewtree Farm (132516) and continue south on a fine flinty track, keeping straight ahead through the woods on Ranmore Common for ¾ mile (1.2km).

Ranmore Common

For centuries Ranmore Common was open heath where local commoners had the right to graze their animals. Once domestic economies no longer relied on the house cow, pig or goose, the common quickly became overgrown with scrub. Now it is a broad, loose-knit wood of oak, yew, holly and birch, famous for bluebells in early summer and protected by the National Trust.

The section of bridleway shown on the maps running due south between OS grid reference 132509 and the road at OS grid reference 132504 has vanished among the trees. Simply keep ahead on the obvious track through the wood to cross the road in a dip (133504). Turn right for 250 yards (250m), then bear left down a broad woodland ride (notice prohibiting motorbikes, cars and horse-drawn wagons). In 300 yards (300m) turn left along the North Downs Way (NDW) at OS grid reference 132500.

North Downs Way

This beautiful old flinty trackway, the oldest road in England, has been hammered out by the tread of beasts and men over at least 5,000 years – maybe much more. It keeps a sheltered and concealed course just below the crests of the ridges and hills. In all it runs for 250 miles (400km), under various guises and names, from Devon to Kent. The eastern half of the trackway between Farnham in Surrey and the Kentish coast is designated the North Downs Way National Trail. Another ancient trackway, the

Pilgrims' Way from Winchester, runs in the valley just below Ranmore Common. Medieval pilgrims in their millions – including Geoffrey Chaucer's *Canterbury Tales* travellers – trod or rode the Pilgrims' Way to the shrine of St Thomas à Becket in Canterbury Cathedral. For some stretches it interweaves with the North Downs Way ridge track. Some call the ancient ridgeway the Harrow Way, or Hoary Way – the Old Road. Bronze Age tin merchants probably used it; so did traders, drovers, warriors and packhorsemen. Now its sole use is as a leisure footpath and bridleway, a grandstand for views such as the one you enjoy as you walk – across the valley and wooded downs, over the roofs, towers and spires of Dorking.

Entering Steers Field (140503) do not aim for the church spire ahead, but aim slightly right of it, keeping the contour for 200 yards (200m); then follow NDW signs to a road (143504). Cross, following the 'Parish Church' sign, to pass St Bartholomew's Church on your right (146505). It was built in 1850 by Thomas Cubitt, builder of much of Victorian London. Cubitt faced St Bartholomew's in striking round flint cobbles, and did not neglect to add a tremendous spire which soon acquired the nickname of 'Cubitt's Finger'. Inside, a dignified little chapel is a memorial to the three sons of Lord and Lady Ashcombe – the brothers were all killed during World War I. Continue along the road from the church. In ⅓ mile (0.5km), where the road bends left outside the gates of Denbies House (151506), keep ahead; in 30 yards (30m) turn right (NDW fingerpost), then left along the North Downs Way. Pass through large estate gates, and keep the contour along a steep hillside above the Denbies vineyard – a fairly recent venture on this south-facing slope. There is a great view ahead to Box Hill rising high on the horizon.

The track swings left to enter woods (158507). Cross a bridlepath (158512); in 250 yards (250m) the North Downs Way bears downhill to the right (159514), but bear left here (FP fingerpost). In 300 yards (300m) bear right along a drive, down to the road by Westhumble Chapel.

Westhumble Chapel

A flint-built west gable with a crude circular central window and a narrow upper window accounts for most of what is left of the little chapel founded for the Westhumble villagers in the late 12th century. By the time of the Reformation it was already disused. At various times it saw service as a barn, and when the railway was being built in the 19th century, the chapel saw congregations once more in the rough forms of the railway navvies.

From the chapel, turn right along the road to reach Boxhill and Westhumble Station.

SHERE, NORTH DOWNS WAY, ST MARTHA-ON-THE-HILL & PILGRIMS' WAY

Two ancient trackways run east–west along the valley of the Tilling Bourne, their parallel courses ½ mile (0.75km) apart – the old droving route that now carries the North Downs Way National Trail high along the chalk ridge of the North Downs and the Pilgrims' Way track through the valley at the feet of the downs. Heading out west along the high road and coming back by the low road, your walk is book-ended by notable churches. You'll visit 'Surrey's prettiest village' in Shere, while fabulous far views are to be had from Newlands Corner high on the downs. A poignant old fable is based around the limpid waters of Silent Pool in the valley below. Add beautiful woodland and meadows, and you have a truly delectable walk in prospect.

Start & Finish:	Gomshall Station
Length of walk:	10½ miles (17km)
OS maps:	1:50,000 Landranger 187; 1:25,000 Explorer 145
Travel:	By rail from London Waterloo (1 hr); by road – M25 (Jct 10), A3, A247, A25.
Features:	St James's Church and the village of Shere; North Downs Way ancient trackway; views from Newlands Corner; Church of St Martha-on-the-Hill; Pilgrims' Way ancient trackway; Silent Pool; Catholic and Apostolic Church, Albury.
Refreshments:	White Horse PH, Shere; New Barn Coffee Shop, Newlands Corner.

THE WALK

From Gomshall Station (089478) cross the A25 (Station Road) and go under the railway line to turn right down Wonham Way. At the sharp left bend in 250 yards (250m) turn right (087475); in another 250 yards (250m) turn right and pass under the railway again. Bear left along the lane to a triangular crossroads (082476); go across into Gravelpits Lane, and in 100 yards (100m) bear right by Gravelpits Farm house into a lane going west across fields. In ⅓ mile (0.5km) turn right through a gate (076477) to reach St James's Church in Shere (074478).

St James's Church and Shere village

St James's Church is a beautiful Norman building. The lychgate was designed by Sir Edwin Lutyens, perfectly framing the Norman tower under its broach spire. A heavy old gallery at the west end is the prelude to a plain, whitewashed interior. There is some lovely 14th-century glass – hawks, animals and foliage – and a really exquisite tiny 13th-century statuette of the Virgin and Child in bronze, which was retrieved by chance from a bramble bush by a dog. It might have been part of a crozier, or perhaps it fell from the staff of some medieval penitent travelling the Pilgrims' Way through the village.

Behind the altar are traces of a 12th-century fresco – foliage and tracery in red ochre round one of the window splays. A little 14th-century quatrefoil window in the chancel was inserted so that the Anchoress of Shere, Christine Carpenter, could view the saying of the Mass. This holy nun was incarcerated in a narrow cell in the church wall at her own request in 1329. She forced her way out at one point, to 'run about, being torn to pieces by attacks of the Tempter'. But after sorrowfully petitioning the bishop of Winchester to be allowed to resume her vocation, she was locked up in prayerful isolation in her cramped cell once more.

Shere is a gorgeous village, threaded by the sparklingly clear Tilling Bourne stream, its lanes lined with fascinating old houses. Look for Bill and Ben the Flowerpot Men in a cottage garden, the old brick-and-flint village lockup with its barred window overlooking the stream, and any number of crooked houses of great charm.

From the church, walk forward to turn right opposite the White Horse pub. Turn left at the T-junction (073479) onto Upper Street, and in 20 yards (20m) turn right up the side of Shere recreation ground. Go under the A25, and bear immediately left up a zigzag path, then right on a track up the left side of Netley Plantation for ½ mile (0.75km) to Hollister Farm

(073490). Keep ahead here to reach a road at the crest of the downs (072494). Turn left on the road and follow the NDW and blue arrow fingerposts for 200 yards (200m), with pastures on your right. Veer right onto the North Downs Way National Trail, following it for 1¾ miles (2.75km) to Newlands Corner (044492).

North Downs Way: the old road to Newlands Corner

The North Downs Way (see pages 105–12 and 147–155) bears the slithery boot-sole prints of modern-day secular pilgrims who tramp this ancient route for pleasure. The way lies along the course of the oldest road in Britain, the Hoary ('Ancient') or Harrow Way, used by drovers and itinerant traders for many millennia before Thomas à Becket's sainthood drew religious penitents to Canterbury. This is a wide old road with broad verges, snaking through dark groves of yew and holly at the top of the downs, keeping just to the south of the crest, combining maximum shelter and view with minimum exposure to unfriendly eyes. Things are quiet along the old road, with very little noise unless a high wind is rushing through the beech tops.

At Newlands Corner enormous views open out – south across the Tilling Bourne valley and the greensand hills of Surrey and Sussex towards the South Downs and north over chalk downland slopes into the low-lying clay basin of London and the Thames Valley. There must be 50 miles (80km) of country in view. Chalkhill flowers, butterflies and birds abound, thanks to the conservation policy of letting sheep and cattle graze this open grassland.

Follow the yellow NDW signs across open downland for ¾ mile (1.2km) to cross White Lane (033490), and turn left downhill on a path alongside the lane. At the bottom of the lane keep ahead by a black-and-white cottage (034486), following NDW signs through the wood, to turn right (032484) on a broad track marked with 'chapel logo' waymarks which climbs St Martha's Hill to the church on the summit (028483).

St Martha-on-the-Hill

The cruciform church, built of rough chunks of dark clinkery ironstone with yellow sandstone facings, stands among dark pine trees at the very summit of its ironstone knoll, a sombre monument. Fragments of the Norman structure built in honour of St Thomas à Becket can still be made

Opposite: The Norman Church of St James in Shere operated as a resting station, waymark and place of physical and spiritual refreshment for medieval pilgrims making their way to the shrine of St Thomas à Becket at Canterbury.

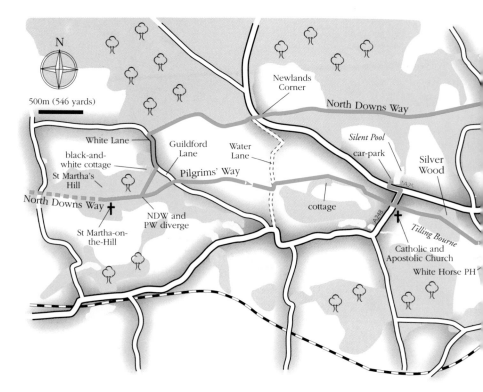

out. The church's dedication to St Martha, the only such dedication in Britain, is probably a centuries-old corruption of 'Martyr's Chapel'. But maybe 'martyr' does not refer to St Thomas at all; there is an account of 600 early Christians being massacred for their faith here. Some say that Martha herself, sister of Mary Magdalene, visited the hill in the company of her brother Lazarus and Joseph of Arimathea. Joseph, a devout follower of Christ, was almost certainly a Phoenician tin trader who might well have known of the Harrow Way. He may even have been Jesus's uncle. Some stories tell of a journey he made to England, bringing his young nephew with him. And did those feet, in ancient time, walk upon England's mountains green...?

From the church retrace your steps to pass the point where the NDW branches off to the left (032484). From this point on you are following the Pilgrims' Way (PW).

Pilgrims' Way

Though the pilgrims travelling to and from Canterbury tended to use the

ancient Harrow Way track, they preferred, where possible, to do what their distant ancestors could not safely do – travel along the valley floors, where there was more shelter from the weather and more water. Settlements with their promise of provisions, beds and warm inns were thicker on the ground, too. The old track just up the slope from the Tilling Bourne was probably in use long before the pilgrims began to pass through the valley, but they certainly used it in their thousands, year by year.

From the NDW junction, keep ahead along the Pilgrims' Way. In 30 yards (30m) pass an old World War II pillbox defensive emplacement on your left and steer ahead, following the wood posts. In 200 yards (200m), at a marker post with bull's head, dragonfly and other waymarks (035485), bear left to a car-park and Guildford Lane. Turn right, and in 50 yards (50m) turn left ('bull's head' waymark and PB fingerpost) along the Pilgrims' Way for ²/₃ mile (1km). Cross Water Lane (047484 – 'bull's head' and PB blue arrow) and continue on the Pilgrims' Way for ¹/₃ mile (0.5km) to a cottage (053485). Bear right here ('Silent Pool' FP marker); in 50 yards (50m) fork right (FP fingerpost and arrow) through the trees, crossing a sandpit road (056484) to reach the A248 (060482) just opposite the Catholic and Apostolic Church, Albury.

Catholic and Apostolic Church, Albury

This grand, overblown church with its pinnacles, big octagonal chapel, imposing north porch and tall graceful windows is, sadly, disused and decaying. It was built in the 1840s for Henry Drummond of Albury Park, who had joined an extreme Christian sect known as the Catholic and Apostolic Faith. The sect was founded by Drummond's charismatic friend Edward Irving, a magnetic presence who believed that the Second Coming of Christ was about to take place. Irving would preach and prophesy for hours on end to congregations of thousands in his Regent Square chapel in London. The squire of Albury fell deeply under his spell. Eventually the hellfire preacher was tried for heresy, and the Catholic and Apostolic Faith fizzled out. William Cobbett, scourge of all humbugs and exploitative landlords, thought Henry Drummond a good and sincere man. Instead of wanting to hang miscreants, Drummond would take them into his service and try to reform them. 'If this be true', remarked Cobbett in *Rural Rides*, 'I know of no man in England so worthy of his estate'.

Turn left up the A248 (there is a footpath on the right side of the hedge) to reach the A25, where you turn left for 100 yards (100m) to cross the dual carriageway (take great care!) into a car-park. A path leads from here to Sherbourne Pond and Silent Pool (061486).

The legend of Silent Pool

This beautiful clear pool, fed by chalk springs and romantically overhung by trees, is the setting for a legend of innocence betrayed, voyeurism and death by drowning. On a lovely day in 1193, young Emma, the woodcutter's beautiful daughter, was enjoying a naked bathe in Silent Pool. Unknown to the maiden, she was being spied on by wicked Prince John, who had come to see for himself if rumours of her beauty were true. Suddenly Emma became aware of the watching figure. Abashed, she waded deeper into the pool to conceal her nakedness and disappeared beneath the water. Her brother arrived, jumped in to try to save her and they drowned in each other's arms. Emma haunts the pool on moonlit nights, when she may be seen bathing and heard to scream as she slips beneath the water.

The legend of Silent Pool is not quite as old as it sounds: it was made up in Victorian times by local doggerel-scribbler Martin Turner. But there is another tale involving the royal rogue John which seems to ring a little more true. The story says that in his youth he stole the girlfriend of Stephen Langton, a youth who lived near Silent Pool. The cuckolded lover had his revenge many years later in 1215, when, as Cardinal Langton, he was one of those who stripped King John of many of his powers by forcing him to sign the first Bill of Rights, Magna Carta.

From Silent Pool return to the Pilgrims' Way (turn left just before the Catholic and Apostolic Church). Follow it across the A248, crossing a stile to continue across another field and through Silver Wood. Leave the wood (066480) to cross a field and go through a windbreak of trees to reach a lane (069478). Cross the lane, and continue along the path for 100 yards (100m) to an intersection. Turn right down the lane signposted 'Ford, 200 Yds'. Continue for 1/3 mile (0.5km) to the crossroads beside the White Horse pub in Shere. From here, retrace your steps to Gomshall Station.

WANBOROUGH, COMPTON & THE HOG'S BACK

One physical feature dominates this walk in west Surrey – the Hog's Back, a long, slim ridge of chalk along whose spine rushes the traffic on the high-perched A31 dual carriageway. Three lovely villages lie below the Hog's Back: tiny Wanborough to the north, Puttenham and Compton to the south. The walk links all three and their historic churches and houses. At Compton you'll find the Watts Gallery, purpose-designed in 1904 to showcase the paintings, drawings and sculpture of the singular Victorian artist George Frederic Watts, and the Memorial Chapel, designed in high Arts and Crafts style by Watts's wife Mary.

Start & Finish:	Wanborough Station
Length of walk:	7 miles (11km)
OS maps:	1:50,000 Landranger 186; 1:25,000 Explorer 145
Travel:	By rail from London Waterloo (1 hr approx.) NB Wanborough Station is closed on Sundays; by road – M3 (Jct 4), A331, A31 towards Guildford, minor road to Wanborough Station (or begin the walk at Wanborough Great Barn).
Features:	Wanborough Great Barn, Wanborough Manor and St Bartholomew's Church; the Hog's Back; Puttenham village; St Nicholas's Church, Watts Memorial Chapel and Watts Gallery at Compton.
Refreshments:	Good Intent PH and Jolly Farmer restaurant, Puttenham; Withies PH and Harrow Inn, Compton; Watts Gallery tea-room.

THE WALK

From Wanborough Station (931503) walk up to the main road and turn right. At the first right bend turn left ('Wanborough Youth House' sign), and in 80 yards (80m) go right (932501 – FP fingerpost) over two stiles and along a fenced path. Cross the next field to a three-way fingerpost; keep ahead here with a hedge on your left, crossing a stile (yellow arrow) and another field to its far left corner, where you reach the road at Wanborough (933490). Cross over and turn left along the tarmac path. In 150 yards (150m) cross the road to bear left along a track ('Wanborough Ancient Church and Great Barn' sign).

Wanborough Great Barn, Manor and church
The medieval Great Barn (934489) stands on brick foundations, its black weatherboarded upper parts under a vast acreage of thin red tiles. The barn has seven bays, side aisles and great double doors, and is of very early crown-post construction. Many rebuildings over the years have lent it a well-seasoned, much-used air.

Wanborough Manor, just beyond, is a mellow 17th-century house with three gables and tall chimney clusters. During World War II the extremely brave young men and women of the SOE (Special Operations Executive) came here to be trained for infiltration into Occupied Europe by submarine, small boat, parachute or Lysander light aeroplane. Once there, they did the best they could to wreck Hitler's plans, operating under constant threat of exposure by betrayal or mischance, followed by capture, interrogation and imprisonment with every prospect of torture and death. A modest plaque under the war memorial in the nearby Church of St Bartholomew does them honour with its inscription: 'Remember before God those members of the European Resistance Movement who trained at Wanborough Manor in World War II and served behind enemy lines in special operations, facing loneliness and unknown dangers in the cause of humanity.'

The Hog's Back
Wanborough Great Barn, Manor and church make a beautiful, quintessentially English ensemble in the low-lying farmlands below the chalk ridge of the Hog's Back, which rises some 300 feet (100m) to close the skyline ½ mile (0.75km) to the south. Celtic tribesmen named it 'Og', the Giant's Back, but there is justification for the 'hog', too, with the spine of the ridge bristling like a boar's hackles in an uninterrupted line of trees and bushes.

The A31 Farnham–Guildford road runs as a dual carriageway for 7 miles (11km) along the crown of the Hog's Back, the two carriageways separated by a hedge. Views from each side of the ridge – north over the thickly wooded clay country of the London basin, south towards the North Downs and the Sussex Weald – are superb.

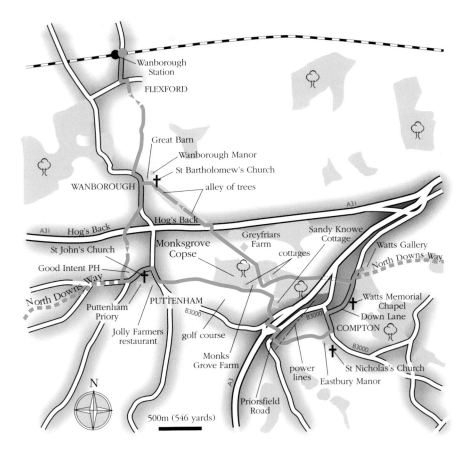

From St Bartholomew's return to the road, cross it (take care!) and turn left up the path for 300 yards (300m) to a left bend in the road (933485). Here a FP fingerpost points up across a field to reach the A31 dual carriageway at the crest of the Hog's Back (931483). Crossing the A31 is perfectly safe, provided you wait patiently until the coast is clear. Cross the Farnham–Guildford carriageway first, next the central reservation hedge between two old yews, and then the Guildford–Farnham carriageway. On the far side, by the entrance to Springfield Manor nursing home, bear right along the side of the A31 for 30 yards (30m), then left (PB fingerpost) down a shady old lane for ¼ mile (0.4km) into Puttenham. Turn left along the road (931478).

Puttenham

Puttenham used to be one of the prime destinations for London's poor East Enders during the September hop-picking season, when the hop farms around the village offered a good fresh-air holiday and the chance to earn a bob or two. Those days are long gone. Now Puttenham is a neat, well-heeled little place. The Good Intent pub, its bar festooned with fragile dried hops, is an excellent village local. Puttenham Priory, on the right of the village road, is a Georgian confection in lemon and white like a rich girl's birthday cake. There are plenty of village houses less grand, but just as comely, too. The church has a stumpy, heavily buttressed tower of rugged stone blocks, and a Norman north arcade with squat round pillars and wavy decoration round the arches. In the churchyard are a couple of good grisly 18th-century skull-and-crossbones graveslabs.

Pass the Good Intent and the church to reach a T-junction (934479). Cross the road and turn right ('Godalming, Compton' sign) along the pavement for 150 yards (150m), then turn left opposite the Jolly Farmer restaurant (NDW fingerpost). This is a rutted old road, sunk between wide hedges of yew, laurel and ivy, in complete contrast to the smoothly shaven fairways and greens of the golf course on its right side. In ¾ mile (1.2km), opposite a row of cottages on your left, a blue bridleway arrow on a post on the right points ahead (947476). At the next blue arrow (948476) turn right along the lane past Sandyknowe Cottage to a T-junction. Turn right for 130 yards (130m), then left across the bridge over the A3 dual carriageway (948472).

On the far side bear right along Priorsfield Road ('Hurtmore, Charterhouse' sign) for 150 yards (150m); then turn left up the bank and over a stile (FP fingerpost). Cross the field, go over another stile and walk beneath power lines to cross a stile by a wood edge (949470). Turn left through bushes and down a sunken lane, past Eastbury Manor. At a PB fingerpost keep ahead along the left side of Eastbury Manor to reach the road in Compton (955471). Turn right to reach St Nicholas's Church (954470).

St Nicholas's Church, Compton

Compton is a special village: not only because of its connection with George Frederic and Mary Watts, leading lights of the Victorian arts scene, but also thanks to the charm of its cottages of brick and flint under tiles

Opposite: *The Watts Memorial Chapel, on its knoll outside Compton, is one of the finest buildings bequeathed by the Arts and Crafts movement of the late 19th century.*

and thatch. St Nicholas's Church is sheltered by a mighty cedar, and its wooden-shingled broad spire stands atop a tower whose windows have a Saxon look about them. Inside are Norman arches with curly-edged patterning and a chancel of unique design – it is split into two storeys, the upper one guarded by a frail wooden arcaded screen of nine bays that has survived from Norman times and is probably the oldest such screen in Britain.

From the church retrace your steps along the road. Just before a T-junction with the B3000, turn right along Down Lane. In 200 yards (200m) turn right through a lychgate to reach the Watts Memorial Chapel (955474).

Watts Memorial Chapel

This extraordinary building of harsh red brick is not George Frederic Watts's mausoleum, as many suppose; it was George and Mary Watts's gift to Compton to mark the opening of the new village cemetery in 1891. Largely designed by Mary Watts, the chapel, with its Greek Cross plan, is a hymn to Arts and Crafts motifs and techniques, from the terracotta celestial orchestra and serene Egyptian handmaidens of the exterior to the doe-eyed angels and solemn cherubim in relief gesso work that adorn the circular interior. It was dismissed as a ridiculous folly for most of the 20th century, but is now recognised as one of the most complete statements of the Arts and Crafts movement. Mary Watts herself was only disappointed in one aspect of the chapel – its cruel red colour.

George Frederic Watts (1817–1904) was driven all his life by the desire to put big, spiritual ideas across in his art. Only in the last decade or so of his life did he receive the recognition he deserved and craved. From 1891 the Wattses lived most of the time at Limnerslease, their house at Compton; and just before George Frederic's death they built and opened a studio there to display his work and that of admired contemporaries.

Watts Gallery

To reach the Watts Gallery, turn right along the road from the chapel; the gallery is on the right in 350 yards (350m). In a series of Arts and Crafts-inspired rooms hang wonderful Watts paintings: portraits such as the heavy-lidded beauty Virginia Countess Somers and the canny, craggy old Earl of Shrewsbury; admonitory biblical scenes (*Eve Repentant*, with Eve slumped in despair against a blasted tree); genre pictures like *The Wounded Heron*; and passionate works such as *The Irish Famine* (a desperate, bedraggled couple with their dying or dead babe), and the huge, dramatic *Time, Death and Justice*, in which Watts overturned convention by depicting both Time and Death as young and beautiful.

Mary Watts's pioneering work is represented, too, with such items as a big gesso altarpiece in which the Crucifixion is transformed into a triumphant Resurrection, the Cross into a blooming Tree of Life. The party pieces, though, are the giant original models for Watts's best-known sculptures, *Tennyson* (the bronze cast now stands outside Lincoln Cathedral) and *Physical Energy* (its bronze is in Kensington Gardens). The huge, vigorous horse and rider of the latter work are tremendously impressive. The model stands on a wheeled trolley, so that it could be pushed out into the open for the public to admire on fine days.

From the gallery, return along the road for 75 yards (75m), and turn right along the North Downs Way (NDW fingerpost). It passes under the B3000, then the A3. At the gate of Monk's Hatch a blue arrow points left as the North Downs Way skirts the property and continues through trees to reach the row of cottages on the right. Turn right off the North Downs Way here (947477 – FP fingerpost on left of NDW), down the right side of Monks Grove Farm. Cross a golf course and follow yellow arrows to the top of Monksgrove Copse (946479). Bear diagonally left here across waste ground, and cross a stile (yellow arrow). Continue diagonally across the next field to cross another stile into the drive of Greyfriars Farm. Cross the drive and the next stile, then continue with a hedge on your right, up two fields to reach the A31 on the Hog's Back (941483).

Cross the first carriageway, then cross the central reservation by a tarmac strip. Cross the second carriageway, and walk left along the far verge for a few yards; then slope down to the right, away from the road (PB fingerpost), along an alley of trees.

Secret tunnel

This is a remarkable ½ mile (0.75km) of trackway (941484 to 934489) across the fields to Wanborough. It must be several hundred years old at least, judging by the maturity of its over-arching hedges of laurel, yew, privet, spindle and elder. You pass along the old lane unseen, walking in a secret leafy tunnel from the rushing road to the quiet old hamlet.

At the Great Barn in Wanborough, bear left to the road and retrace your outward walk to reach Wanborough Station.

LISS, SELBORNE & HANGERS WAY

This long day's walk in Hampshire's glorious countryside takes you to Selborne, an enchanting village forever associated with its 18th-century curate, Gilbert White, whose *Natural History and Antiquities of Selborne* became one of the best-selling books ever written. You can visit White's house, The Wakes, which also contains an exhibition devoted to Lawrence Oates, Antarctic explorer and self-sacrificial hero. Other delights of the walk include two fascinating village churches, gorgeous (although muddy) bridlepaths through the beech-woods, and old-fashioned sunken lanes that are a real pleasure to ramble in.

Start & Finish:	Liss Station
Length of walk:	15 miles (24km)
OS maps:	1:50,000 Landranger 186; 1:25,000 Explorer 133
Travel:	By rail from London Waterloo (1hr 5 mins); by road – M25 (Jct 10), A3.
Features:	Sunken lanes and beech-woods; Church of the Holy Rood, Empshott; Gilbert White's House and the Lawrence Oates Museum at The Wakes, Selborne; Gilbert White's grave and other White-related sites around Selborne; the Zig-Zag and the Hanger; Selborne Common; Holtham Lane and Button's Lane; Church of St Peter and St Paul, Hawkley.
Refreshments:	Queen's Hotel and Selborne Arms, Selborne; Hawkley Inn, Hawkley.

THE WALK

From Liss Station (777277), cross the railway level crossing and walk up the village street. Turn left into the churchyard, and go through the gap in the hedge to the right of the church (775279). Continue along the right side

Opposite: A detail from a very fine stained-glass window in St Mary's Church, Selborne, honours the much-loved writer and village curate Gilbert White.

of the field and through a kissing gate to cross a road. Carry on along a green lane to cross another road (771284 – 'Liss' sign and FP fingerpost), up steps and on. In 100 yards (100m) turn left over a stile (yellow arrow) and skirt the graveyard of West Liss church, aiming for the far corner of a field (FP fingerpost). Go through a gate and cross the A3 dual carriageway by a bridge. Go through the gate on the far side and keep ahead (FP fingerpost and yellow arrow). In 150 yards (150m) cross a stile, and aim slightly left to cross a stile by a gate (764286). Go along the field edge with the hedge on your left; opposite Berrygrove Farm cross a stile, and continue to cross two more stiles into a green lane. In 200 yards (200m) turn right (758288), and follow the fenced path round to the left over a stile (FP fingerpost). In 100 yards (100m) cross another stile (757289), and turn left along a wide green lane.

In 200 yards (200m) turn right over a stile (FP fingerpost) and up a fenced path on the left edge of a field. Just before the yard of Scotland Farm go left over a stile (755291 – FP fingerpost). A fenced path takes you round the top edge of one field and the bottom edge of the next to a road, where you turn left and walk steeply uphill through a belt of trees. Pass Uplands, and at the following left bend turn right (750295 – PB fingerpost) through a gate. Follow the bridleway round the right edge of a field; in 300 yards (300m) bear right (PB fingerpost) down tree-root 'steps' to turn right along a sunken lane. In 100 yards (100m) the lane forks by Mabbotts house, keep ahead on the level along Standfast Lane.

Sunken lanes

The sunken lanes of east Hampshire are beautiful, if extremely muddy, and Standfast Lane is no exception. The hooves and feet of the centuries have worn a deep channel in the soft clay and chalk of the fields. The banks are mossy and well grown with field maple and hazel interspersed with large ash and beech trees. In spring there are drifts of violets and primroses in the hedge roots, and there always seems to be a light trickle of bird song flowing from the woods.

After 1/3 mile (0.5km) go through a gate; in another 125 yards (125m) turn left over a stile (755305 – FP fingerpost) along a ride running west between two woodlands. In 200 yards (200m) cross a stile, and keep ahead with a wood close on your left. Cross two more stiles; then, within sight of a house, bear right (yellow arrows) over a stile to cross a stream. Climb the bank to cross a stile into Mill Lane (750307 – FP fingerpost). Turn right into Empshott. As you enter the village, turn right to reach the Church of the Holy Rood (753313).

SELBORNE

St Mary's Church

The Wakes

The Queen's Hotel

Selborne Arms PH

The Zig-Zag

Selborne Common

Green Lane

Tawny Barn

High Wood Hanger

Holtham Lane

NOAR HILL

Church of the Holy Rood

Hangers Way

EMPSHOTT

Button's Lane

Mill Lane

Vann Farm

Standfast Lane

Mabbotts house

bear right down tree-root steps

Hawkley Inn

Uplands

Church of St Peter and St Paul

Scotland Farm

green lane

Hawkley Hanger

West Liss Church

HAWKLEY

Hangers Way

climb bank and cross stile

Liss Station

Berrygrove Farm

green lane

LISS

N

500m (546 yards)

Church of the Holy Rood, Empshott

Holy Rood is a lovely early 13th-century church, set on a knoll looking out over woods. It is full of curiosities and delights – side aisles so narrow that you can hardly squeeze between the nave arcade and the outer walls; ornate Victorian woodwork up in the roof; two fine William Kemp windows (St Michael with large green wings and St George looking as pretty as a young girl in a fur-trimmed cloak); solid, plain medieval pews and Jacobean altar rails.

From the church, return to the road junction and turn right. Just before a T-junction go left (754317 – PB fingerpost) down a field edge, over a fence and up a field slope to cross a stile and turn right inside High Wood Hanger (751317 – FP fingerpost) and walk along its lower edge. The footpath soon becomes a bridleway. Keep along the bottom edge of the wood for nearly a mile (1.6km) to emerge from the trees and bear right (740321 – Hangers Way/HW green arrow waymark) along a chalky trackway to reach a road. Turn right to pass 'Tawny Barn' (named 'Lower Noar Hill Farm' on the Explorer map) and reach a T-junction (739325). Cross a stile and follow a FP fingerpost and HW arrows round two sides of a field and on through squeeze stiles for ¾ mile (1.2km) along field edges and then along a fenced path before following a lane to meet the B3006 by the Selborne Arms in Selborne (742335). Turn left for the Queen's Hotel, The Wakes and St Mary's Church.

Gilbert White and Selborne

Gilbert White (1720–1793), curate of Selborne, possessed a pair of sharp eyes and an open, enquiring mind. Everything was grist to his intellectual mill, from the orgasms of swifts to the submersible breathing apparatus of deer. He was among the first to infer the annual migration of swallows. White was operating on the cusp between the Age of Reason and the Age of Romance, and memorably blended tender emotion and precise scientific observation in his writings on the natural world as it went about its affairs around Selborne. The volume containing his letters to correspondents Daines Barrington and Thomas Pennington, published in 1788 as *The Natural History and Antiquities of Selborne*, has sold countless millions of copies and drawn innumerable admirers all over the world under the spell of the obscure country curate and his few miles of Hampshire.

The Wakes

White's lifelong home, The Wakes, is now a very well-run museum. The garden, with the ha-ha that White built, contains many of the species of plants that the curate enthused over and cared for. When The Wakes was up for sale in the 1950s it proved too expensive for Gilbert White devotees to buy; but the purchaser, Robert Washington Oates, allowed the house to function as a Gilbert White museum on condition that his own ancestor, Captain Lawrence Oates of the Antarctic, should also be honoured with a permanent exhibition. So there is an incongruous but fascinating Oates section, commemorating the bravery of the explorer who hauled his frostbitten, gangrenous body out of the Scott expedition tent on 17 March 1912, going into the blizzard to die alone with the immortally heroic words: 'I am just going outside. I may be some time.'

St Mary's Church, Selborne
Across the road you'll find St Mary's Church. Gilbert White's grave is discreetly indicated in the graveyard, north of the chancel. Inside St Mary's are two beautiful stained-glass windows in memory of the curate – one showing St Francis feeding a splendid collection of birds, and the other featuring three roundels with rather anthropomorphised creatures.

From St Mary's Church, return up the village street to the Selborne Arms and turn right, passing a National Trust 'Selborne Common Footpath Only' sign, then a 'Footpath to the Zig Zag and Hanger' fingerpost.

The Zig-Zag and Selborne Common
Climb the Zig-Zag, a back-and-forth path which rises 270 feet (80m) up the face of Selborne Hanger. The 28 zigs and zags were cut by Gilbert White and his brother in 1753. From the seat at the top (741332) there's a splendid view over Selborne. Pass the seat and turn right, with a hedge and house on your left. Continue westward on this broad path into the trees and across Selborne Common. The Common, one of Gilbert White's favourite places, is a superb open area of beech-wood, oak and bracken administered by the National Trust – almost 250 acres (110ha) of tangly wild land.

The path runs for ³/₄ mile (1.2km) across Selborne Common. After just over ¹/₂ mile (0.75km) it forks by an upright but sawn-off tree trunk; bear left here, and in 300 yards (300m) reach the western edge of the common (729328). Turn left (PB fingerpost), and in 10 yards (10m) keep ahead (another PB fingerpost). The track gains the map name of Green Lane, then reaches a road (731322). Turn right, and after 150 yards (150m) go over a crossroads; in 150 yards (150m) bear left (728320) along a green lane for 2 miles (3.25km), crossing a road at OS grid reference 728306.

Holtham Lane and Button's Lane

This is another really fine green lane, metamorphosing from Holtham Lane into Button's Lane as it curves in a C-shape through the uplands. It is hedged by gnarled pollarded oaks, field maples and beeches, interspersed with thick blocks of holly. Leaves carpet it in parts; other stretches are stony, boggy or grassy. As Button's Lane descends towards Vann Farm, the deep channel gouged down the centre tells of its annual winter transformation into a torrent.

Where Button's Lane meets a road (739307), turn right to pass Vann Farm and its duck pond; then turn right over a stile (Hangers Way/HW fingerpost), up a field edge with a hedge on your right. Cross a stile (HW) and aim for the top right corner of this field. Bear left here (737306 – FP fingerpost and HW) along a field edge with a hedge on your right. At the far end of the field cross a stile (HW); descend steps to cross a footbridge, then ascend to bridleway fingerposts. Keep ahead (HW) on a track along the bottom edge of Hawkley Hanger. Opposite Hawkley church tower, where the path swings sharply right, go left (740290 – PB fingerpost and HW) along field edges to the road in Hawkley (745290). Turn left to the church.

Church of St Peter and St Paul, Hawkley

Hawkley's Church of St Peter and St Paul was completely rebuilt in 1865, but is an excellent example of how the Victorians sometimes got their country churches right. There are chunky, cylindrical columns in the nave arcades, their capitals richly carved. Floral corbels support the nave roof and angels embellish the aisles. Later generations have had their influence, too. The south chapel is beautified by a marvellous late 20th-century mural of local flowers, birds and animals by Sally Maltby, illuminating the theme: 'I will lift up mine eyes unto the hills'.

Leaving the church, bear left up the road past the Hawkley Inn to a T-junction (749299). Turn right here ('West Liss 1½' sign) along the road. Go round a sharp left-hand hairpin bend, and in 40 yards (40m) climb the bank on your right and cross a stile (751287 – FP fingerpost). Aim left for the bottom left corner of the field to cross a stile into another field; again, aim left for a stile in the bottom left corner of the field; cross the stile onto a road (755288). Turn right and then immediately left along a green lane; this will return you to the stile at OS grid reference 759289 (see outward journey, page 172). Turn right to cross the stile, and retrace your steps past Berrygrove Farm to Liss.

OVERTON, HANNINGTON & WATERSHIP DOWN

A tremendous roof-of-the-world walk that lasts all day and will leave you tired but happy, with a mind full of gorgeous downland scenes. You start in the lovely valley of the River Test amid the tree-hung reservoirs of long-defunct paper mills. A long stretch of old chalk-and-flint trackways brings you north to Hannington and its pretty church and village green, then on to the dramatic north-facing escarpment of Watership Down. Thoughts around here are of Bigwig, Fiver, Hazel and the other rabbits, whose adventures in Richard Adams's classic tale *Watership Down* were set on these uplands. Long tracks across the downs bring you south again, crossing an old Roman road running forgotten in a strip of woodland, to reach the oldest road in Britain and more scenes from *Watership Down*. From here you descend into the valley of the Test to end your long walk in lowland surroundings once more.

Start & Finish:	Overton Station
Length of walk:	15 miles (24km)
OS maps:	1:50,000 Landranger 185, 1:25,000 Explorer 144
Travel:	By rail from London Waterloo (1 hr); by road – M3 (Jct 8), A303 and minor roads to Overton.
Features:	Mill pools at Overton; barn at Manor Farm, North Oakley; etched windows by Laurence Whistler in All Saints' Church, Hannington; *Watership Down* scenes; downland views and tracks; Portway Roman road in Caesar's Belt; Harrow Way ancient trackway.
Refreshments:	Vine Inn, Hannington.

THE WALK

Overton was founded by Bishop Lucy of Winchester in 1217 to provide His Grace with cash from rents. The Hampshire town beside the River Test became the site of a great sheep fair; up to 50,000 animals would be driven to the pastures by the river to be sold. Milling was big business, too – flour milling at first, then silk production and, finally, paper for bank notes. The legacy left by the mills is a long run of ponds, which snake from near the source of the river on down the valley. They make a picturesque accompaniment to the start of the walk.

From Overton Station (518508) walk down Station Road, with brick cottages on your right. Keep ahead at a junction, and in 80 yards (80m) turn left (519504 – small 'Polhampton' sign). In ¼ mile (0.4km), where the road bends right to cross the River Test (523505), keep ahead ('No Through Road' sign). In another ¼ mile (0.4km), beside a cottage with five dormer windows on your left (526507), bear left up a green lane, under the railway and onto a road (526512). Turn right along this quiet country lane for ¾ mile (1.2km), crossing a lane (532515) to reach a T-junction near Ashe Warren Farm (536520). A 'Right of Way' fingerpost points on along a green lane for another mile (1.6km).

Country lanes of the Hampshire Downs

These country lanes of the Hampshire downs – both the tarmac motor roads and the green lanes – are remarkably quiet. You can walk for hours and see only a handful of cars on the tarred lanes, while other walkers are a rarity. This is country-lane rambling as it used to be before rural roads got crowded and drivers forgot how to go slowly and patiently.

Just before reaching cottages on White Lane, the Wayfarer's Walk (WW) trail crosses the green road. Turn left here over a stile (551526 – FP fingerpost and WW green arrow) along a path, bearing left in 50 yards (50m) in the outer skirt of a hazel wood. Follow WW arrows on a clear track for ¾ mile (1.2km) to Freemantle Farm. Bear left through the farmyard (543537 – FP fingerpost and WW), and in 300 yards (300m) turn right (FP fingerpost and WW arrows) through a hedge and diagonally left across a field, aiming for the thatched barn at the Manor Farm, North Oakley (538541).

Manor Farm barn

This is a lovely old building, a Tudor barn with a really fine hammerbeam roof which would grace any country church. And the barn, being still in full use, has the dignity of employment to add to the patina of centuries and

Opposite: Beech hangers ride the edge of the Watership Down escarpment under enormous billowing skies – heavenly countryside for rabbits and ramblers alike.

the rugged strength and beauty of its construction. North Oakley is a tiny hamlet caught in a fold of the downs among large open fields of pale flinty soil, good clumps of woodland and patches of grass where hares lollop.

Turn right along the road, rounding a left bend to walk up to the hilltop village of Hannington. The Vine (540553) is a fine inn on the southern edge of the village; beyond it lies the village green, where the head of the village well is still protected by a miniature tiled broach spire that was installed to commemorate Queen Victoria's 1897 Diamond Jubilee. Beyond the well stands All Saints' Church (539555).

All Saints' Church, Hannington

The little crooked flint All Saints' Church raises its broach spire among limes and yews; a plain village church, rather barn-like, with a blocked north door and a large weather-beaten Mass dial. The church is graced by two extremely beautiful engraved windows. One shows a sheaf of corn, a flock of sheep on the downs with a sheepdog intently watching them, a sunburst lighting up the scene and a shadowy scythe; it is inscribed 'Remember William Whistler, farmer, 1886–1978'. The other window, to Rose Hodson, shows a crucifix rising above a house. Rose tendrils climb from a chimney and a window to wrap themselves round the Cross and change it into a Tree of Life. 'Lord who shall dwell in thy tabernacle, or who shall rest upon thy holy hills?' asks the inscription. 'What if Earth be but the shadow of Heaven and things therein, each to other like?'

The path passes down the right side of the church and doglegs round a barn. In 20 yards (20m) ignore a stile and FP fingerpost on your right (537555) and keep ahead with a hedge on your left to go through a wicket gate. Follow the field edge, on a path between hedges, to go through the hedge at the top of For Down (531553). To your right a line of electricity poles crosses the next field, while a FP fingerpost points ahead. Take a westerly line that bisects this angle; look for a pylon seen on the skyline just to the left of the electricity poles and aim a little to the left of this. Steer past the right-hand edge of an old chalk hollow that appears ahead, to pass through a gap in the hedge on the far side of the field (526554 – FP fingerposts and WW). Here you rejoin the Wayfarer's Walk as you turn right along a drive to a road. Turn left for 25 yards (25m), then right along a green lane ('Right of Way' fingerpost and WW). Pass under power lines, and continue for ¾ mile (1.2km) to cross the B3051 at the crest of White Hill (516565).

Continue along WW for 1¼ miles (2km) until you arrive opposite the northern end of Cannon Avenue beech hanger (499569) on Watership Down.

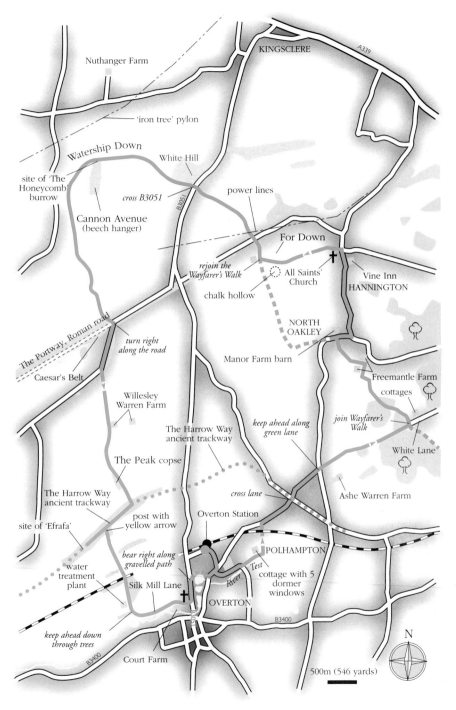

Nuthanger Farm

KINGSCLERE

A339

'iron tree' pylon

Watership Down

White Hill

site of 'The Honeycomb' burrow

cross B3051

B3051

power lines

Cannon Avenue
(beech hanger)

For Down

rejoin the
Wayfarer's Walk

All Saints'
Church

Vine Inn
HANNINGTON

chalk hollow

NORTH
OAKLEY

The Portway, Roman road

turn right
along the road

Caesar's Belt

Manor Farm barn

Freemantle Farm
cottages

Willesley
Warren Farm

The Harrow Way
ancient trackway

keep ahead along
green lane

join Wayfarer's
Walk

White Lane

The Peak copse

The Harrow Way
ancient trackway

cross lane

Ashe Warren Farm

site of 'Efrafa'

post with
yellow arrow

Overton Station

POLHAMPTON

water
treatment
plant

bear right along
gravelled path

River Test

cottage with 5
dormer
windows

Silk Mill Lane

B3051

OVERTON

B3400

keep ahead down
through trees

B3400

Court Farm

500m (546 yards)

N

181

Scenes from Watership Down

Richard Adams, author of the celebrated novel *Watership Down*, grew up hereabouts and knew this beautiful grassy down well. To amuse his daughters on long car drives he began to spin them yarns about a group of rabbits who lived in a burrow on Watership Down. The tale grew to become a full-length novel, meticulously observed, beautifully written, humorously told and immensely exciting. It was greeted coolly on first publication in 1972, but when the American public 'discovered' it two years later, *Watership Down* became a worldwide best-seller.

You can identify several of the story's locations from the crest of Watership Down. Cannon Avenue wood is the beech hanger at whose northern edge the rabbits dug their 'Honeycomb' burrow. Walk to the rim of the escarpment, which falls away 260 feet (80m) in a sudden swoop. Up this slope the rabbits toiled on their arrival after a dangerous journey from Sandleford Warren. Later in the book, Blackberry and Dandelion lured the dog from Nuthanger Farm up the escarpment to burst upon the fearsome rabbit villain General Woundwort as he was about to destroy the warren. Nuthanger Farm itself is hidden by a rise of ground below in the valley, but between the farm and the down you can see the 'iron tree' or pylon that features in the tale.

Follow the white railings of racehorse gallops on from Cannon Avenue. Soon they diverge to the right (497568); keep a hedge on your left and follow it round to the left to go through a gate ('Hants County Council Off Road Cycle Trail' arrow). Continue southwards along this track by the hedge for 1¾ miles (2.9km) to pass through the long windbreak wood called Caesar's Belt and reach a road (502543).

Caesar's Belt and the Portway Roman road

Caesar's Belt is a 3-mile (5-km) strip of larch, hazel and beech trees. It conceals the raised causeway of the Portway, a Roman road that ran between the settlement at Old Sarum, just north of present-day Salisbury, and the town of Calleva Atrebatum or Silchester (see pages 186–9). The Portway may have existed as a route for a thousand years before the Romans came to Britain; it is thought that they simply straightened and improved what was already there.

Turn right along the road for ⅓ mile (0.5km), taking great care. At the right bend seen ahead bear left on a farm track (500536) and continue south for a mile (1.6km) past Willesley Warren Farm (501528) and The Peak copse. At the far end of The Peak (504518) keep ahead along a grassy track for ¼ mile (0.4km), to turn right (505515 – BW fingerpost) along the Harrow Way ancient trackway.

The Harrow Way

The Harrow Way can claim to be Britain's oldest road, a trackway whose course can be traced across the whole of southern England in a magnificent 250-mile (420-km) arc from Dorset to the Kentish coast. Tin-traders, farmers, hunters, drovers, warriors and pilgrims have trodden out its course over perhaps five millennia – maybe much longer. Its eastern half is now the very popular North Downs Way National Trail/Pilgrims' Way (see pages 105–12 and 147–69), but here along its western course it is little frequented. It runs 20 yards (20m) wide, carpeted with leaves, flanked by many tree and bush species – sycamore, oak, ash, beech, elder, hazel, yew, larch, cherry, blackthorn, whitethorn, to name but half. The Harrow Way reeks of history and human activity over the centuries – a noble high thoroughfare across the downs, cloaked in the anonymity of its dense hedges.

Follow the Harroway for ¹/₃ mile (0.5km), to pass a post with a yellow arrow pointing left (501511). Continue for ¹/₄ mile (0.4km) to reach a crossing of tracks at a BW fingerpost (498508).

'Efrafa'

Here Richard Adams sited 'Efrafa', the enemy warren that was run with military precision and brutal efficiency by that 'crack-brained slave-driver' Woundwort, as Bigwig styled him. It was here that the Watership Down rabbits came on their hazardous doe-stealing expedition, only just escaping with their lives – and with the females – in one of the tensest episodes in *Watership Down*.

From Efrafa return to the post with the yellow arrow (501511). Bear right to leave the Harrow Way and walk down a field edge with the hedge on your left. Cross a track, go through a belt of trees and then cross the railway (504503 – please take care!) by steep steps. Continue past a water treatment plant and on down a lane for 200 yards (200m). Where it bends right (505498 – yellow arrow on a post) keep ahead down through trees to bear left along Silk Mill Lane for ¹/₃ mile (0.5km). Turn right at a junction (512499). At Court Farm follow the road round to the left to meet the B3051 (515499) by a church. Cross the road and turn left along the pavement; then in 300 yards (300m) bear right (515502 – FP fingerpost) along a gravelled path round a mill reservoir to meet a road (518503). Turn left to reach Overton Station.

STRATFIELD MORTIMER, SILCHESTER ROMAN TOWN & THE DEVIL'S HIGHWAY

This walk follows some fascinating ancient trackways on the Berkshire/Hampshire border, notably the old Roman road long known as the Devil's Highway. You'll walk the Roman walls that encircle the Romano-British city of Calleva Atrebatum, today called Silchester. Lovers of stained glass can admire some beautiful pieces in St Mary's Church at Stratfield Mortimer, while the other St Mary's on the route – built right on Silchester's Roman walls – boasts fine craftsmanship covering 700 years.

Start & Finish:	Mortimer Station
Length of walk:	9 miles (14km)
OS maps:	1:50,000 Landranger 175; 1:25,000 Explorer 159
Travel:	By rail from London Paddington (50 mins approx); by road – A33 (M4, Jct 11), minor roads west from the B3349 at Riseley.
Features:	Saxon graveslab and medieval glass in St Mary's Church, Stratfield Mortimer; 13th-century stonework, 15th-century angel screen, medieval tombs and wall-painting in St Mary's Church, Silchester; Roman amphitheatre and the Roman town of Calleva Atrebatum at Silchester; the Devil's Highway.
Refreshments:	Fox and Horn PH, Stratfield Mortimer; Old Elm Tree PH, Beech Hill.

THE WALK

From Mortimer station (672641) walk up to the road and turn left. In 100 yards (100m) turn left at the mini-roundabout, pass the Fox and Horn pub, and in 250 yards (250m) turn left (669642 – BW fingerpost) to St Mary's Church.

St Mary's Church, Stratfield Mortimer

St Mary's has to be kept locked; the keyholder (for the telephone number, see Further Information, pages 192–201) lives ½ mile (0.75km) away, but it is well worth adding the extra half-hour to your walk in order to see its two ancient treasures.

The Saxon graveslab fixed to the south wall of the chancel is inscribed: 'On the eight before the Kalends of October [24 September], Aegelward son of Kypping was laid in this place. Blessed be the man who prays for his soul. Toki made me'. Toki was the name of one of King Canute's courtiers, which would date this graveslab to about AD 1000.

Go through the little door between the graveslab and the organ to find St Mary's ancient stained glass gathered in a three-light lancet window. These are beautiful fragments. In the central lancet, William of Wykeham, founder of Winchester College, takes centre stage with a many-folded face and his motto 'Manners Maketh Man' inscribed beside him. In the right-hand panel we see Christ labelled 'Salvator Mundi' (Saviour of the World) with a sunburst behind him and a globe in his hand; above him the prodigal son sits despondently under a tree in a farmyard where a herd of pigs is enthusiastically gobbling swill. The left panel is a fine naturalistic scene labelled 'November', showing two yeomen cutting down leafless trees while a centaur in the middle distance bends his bow purposefully.

The path runs along the left side of the churchyard, bearing to the left of a pond and crossing a stile (FP fingerpost). Keep the pond on your right and follow the field edge. In ¼ mile (0.4km) bear right over a footbridge (666637 – FP fingerpost), then turn left with the stream on your left. In 250 yards (250m) ignore a plank footbridge on your left; in another 300 yards (300m) turn left over a stile (664634) and continue in the same direction as before, keeping the stream on your left. At the far end of the field cross a stile (yellow arrow) and follow the left-hand field edge round to the right to cross a stile and reach a road (657632). Turn left. In ¼ mile (0.4km), at a T-junction, bear left past Brocas Lands Farm; at the next left bend keep ahead (653630) along a green lane. In 250 yards (250m) ignore the FP fingerpost on your right to follow the lane for ¾ mile (1.2km) to a road.

Green lane

This old green lane is one of those sunken, secret ways through the fields that wind across so much of England's landscape. Walking its rutted channel gives a sense of connection with a distant agricultural past.

Bulbous oaks and field maples line its hedges. It is extremely muddy in parts, and prone to landslips; the sandy, gravelly soil is liable to burst out of the banks and half block the way.

The green lane follows its own logic as to twists and turns; logic obscured nowadays, since the fields and farms it served have shifted their relationships with each other, and their levels of accessibility and importance, since this modest trackway's heyday as a vital local communication route.

At the road (645625), keep ahead for 200 yards (200m) past Manor Farm to find St Mary's Church, Silchester, on your right (643624).

St Mary's Church, Silchester

St Mary's stands right on the Roman wall that encloses the 100-acre (40-ha) site of Calleva Atrebatum, the Romano-British city that the Saxons came to call Silchester. The wall stands over 6 feet (2m) high hereabouts, its flint cobbles and stone laid in layers, herringbone style. St Mary's is a remarkable church; it was built on a site reckoned to be sacred since pagan times, and continues a tradition of Christian worship in this location dating back to a little 4th-century basilica which has been excavated amid the ruins of Calleva Atrebatum.

St Mary's 15th-century chancel screen is exceptional; it contains 15 broad-winged angels, each crouched uncomfortably on a bent left knee. It was hidden in a barn to save it from destruction during the Reformation upheavals, and restored to the church some 300 years later. The red-and-yellow floral designs painted round the chancel windows must date to when the chancel was built around 1230. But St Mary's is not just a museum of medieval art. There are plain but beautiful early 20th-century bench ends carved with biblical plants: palm, apple, olive, mulberry, bulrush, cucumber and more. And over the font hangs a modern wrought-iron corona featuring seeds – or are they crucifixion nails? – bursting into flower.

From the church, follow the path through the churchyard to the north-east corner. Two kissing gates lead to a gravelled lane; turn left to walk across the waist of the site of Calleva Atrebatum. At the far side, turn right through a kissing gate (636625) to walk a half circuit of the Roman walls back to the road by Manor Farm.

Opposite: Silchester's two-mile ring of Roman wall, built of flint, stone and tiles, stands 15 feet (5m) high in places and is reputed to be the finest surviving run of Roman wall in Britain.

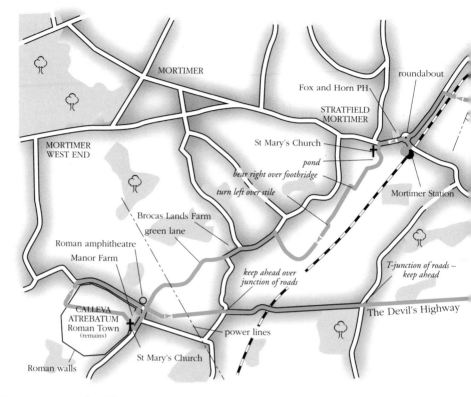

Roman town of Calleva Atrebatum

The walls of Calleva Atrebatum, made of flint with stone courses, were built around AD 270, and their ring of almost 2 miles (3.2km) is reckoned to be the finest run of Roman wall in Britain. They were built to strengthen the earthen ramparts put up here by the Romans shortly after they conquered Britain in the 1st century AD. The Romans superimposed their town of Calleva Atrebatum, 'the place in the woods where the Atrebates dwell', on a settlement of the Atrebates tribe which had been established for at least a century. Not that the Atrebates were themselves locals; they were a Belgic tribe, a warrior aristocracy that had fled to Britain after a failed rising against the Roman occupation of Gaul. Once established here, they lorded it over the local tribes until the coming of the Romans. The Atrebates did not care for quislings; when their own king Commius brought them a message from Julius Caesar ordering them to submit to the 'protection of the Romans', they threw him in prison and loaded him with chains.

Calleva Atrebatum grew to be one of the major Roman garrison towns of southern England. The haphazardly sited Celtic houses were replaced by a

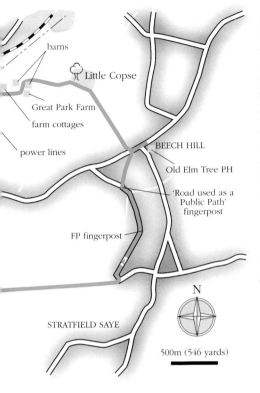

barns

Little Copse

Great Park Farm

farm cottages

power lines

BEECH HILL

Old Elm Tree PH

'Road used as a Public Path' fingerpost

FP fingerpost

STRATFIELD SAYE

N

500m (546 yards)

regular grid of streets. Buildings were at first of timber, but were rebuilt in stone a century or so after the foundation of the Roman town. They included a colonnaded forum, baths, temples, shops, houses, and a large inn with a courtyard – also the Christian church. The town had its own mint, too. Living conditions were spacious, even gracious: houses had an acre of ground to themselves. Artefacts uncovered during the early 20th-century excavation of the town include mosaics, ornamental plasterwork, wooden barrels and buckets, jewellery in bronze and gold, surgical instruments and domestic tools, knives and candlesticks.

Calleva Atrebatum seems to have flourished until the Romans left Britain around AD 410, then limped on until the invading Saxons burned it around AD 500. Some tales say that Aella the Saxon gathered sparrows and sent them into the city with firebrands tied to their tails. Others tell of how King Arthur was crowned at Calleva before its destruction.

Back at the road by Manor Farm, turn left. In 100 yards (100m) go round a left bend to find Calleva's Roman amphitheatre on the right side of the road (645626).

Amphitheatre of Calleva Atrebatum

This large, bowl-shaped, open-air theatre was built between AD 50 and AD 75, at the time of the foundation of Calleva Atrebatum. It, too, started life as an earth-and-timber structure before being rebuilt in stone in the 3rd century AD. The big stone-walled circle with its high, sloped banks was capable of accommodating 3,500 customers seated or 7,000 standing: they would have watched triumphal ceremonies, theatrical spectacles and gladiatorial combat. Judging by the provenance of most of the bones unearthed, horses were the principal victims. The amphitheatre had been abandoned by the time the Romans left Britain.

From the amphitheatre, return to the gate. Bear left to the bend in the road, and go straight ahead to follow the footpath (FP fingerpost) across a field and under power lines. At the far side of the field (653625) keep ahead over a junction of roads, and follow this lane for 1 mile (1.6km). Cross the railway (657625) to reach a T-junction of roads (667626). Cross here and keep ahead along the green lane called the Devil's Highway.

The Devil's Highway

It is the Roman road from Calleva Atrebatum to London that forms the ruler-straight Devil's Highway – a name that reflects local folk memories going back to the Dark Ages, when the crumbling works of the Romans were taken to be so far beyond the capabilities of ordinary men that they must have been made by giants or supernatural beings.

The Devil's Highway is wide, thickly hedged and hugely rutted. In places the ruts are 3 or 4 feet (1m) deep, down to the Roman hardcore, thanks to off-road motorists and their selfish sport. But there are dry, firm verges that skirt the worst bits.

After 1½ miles (2.5km) the Devil's Highway meets a road (692627); turn left here. Pass one FP fingerpost on your right; then take the next right of way on the right (693637 – 'Road Used As Public Path' fingerpost) to reach the road at Beech Hill (693640). Turn right if you want to visit the Old Elm Tree pub; otherwise turn left along the pavement for 50 yards (50m), then turn right (FP fingerpost) to cross a stile and a field. Cross another stile (FP fingerpost) and continue across the next field to go through a gate in the dip (691645). Aim for the nearest corner of the wood ahead; go through the gate (FP fingerpost) and along the left side of Little Copse. Where the wood swings right (687647) keep ahead to cross a stile (yellow arrow); walk across the next field to cross a stile onto a farm track (683647). In 20 yards (20m) cross another stile (yellow arrow); in the far left corner of this field bear left over a gate and walk between the farm buildings of Great Park Farm. Pass the farmhouse and follow the track as it swings right out of the farmyard. In 200 yards (200m) pass farm cottages; keep ahead here over a stile (679646 – yellow arrow) to cross a field under power lines. Cross the railway by stiles (676646) to reach a road. Cross it and turn left along the grass verge into Stratfield Mortimer; at the mini-roundabout bear left to Mortimer Station.

Opposite: The pretty 15th-century Church of St Mary, Silchester, is sited on a spot believed sacred since pagan times, and was a place of Christian worship as far back as the 4th century AD.

FURTHER INFORMATION

GORING & MAPLEDURHAM

King Charles Head PH
Reading Road, Collins End, Goring
Heath, Reading, Oxfordshire
Tel: 01491 680268
Food-serving times: Monday–Thursday
12pm–2.30pm, 6pm–9pm;
Friday 12–2.30pm, 6pm–9.30pm;
all day Sunday.

Mapledurham House, Mill and Tea-room
The Estate Office, Mapledurham
House, Reading, Oxfordshire
Tel: 0118 972 3350
www.mapledurham.co.uk
Opening hours: Easter–September:
Saturday & Sunday 2pm–5pm.

HENLEY-ON-THAMES, GREYS COURT & ROTHERFIELD PEPPARD

Dog Inn
Peppard Common, Henley-on-Thames,
Oxfordshire
Tel: 01491 628343
Food-serving times: Monday–Saturday
11am–10pm; Sunday 12pm–10pm.

Greys Court
Rotherfield Greys, Henley-on-Thames,
Oxfordshire
Tel: 01491 628529/755564
www.nationaltrust.org.uk
Opening hours:
House April–September: Wednesday,
Thursday & Friday 2pm-6pm.
Gardens April–September:
Tuesday–Saturday 2pm–6pm.

Maltsters Arms PH
Rotherfield Greys, Henley-on-Thames,
Oxfordshire
Tel: 01491 628400
Food-serving times: Monday–Saturday
12pm–2.15pm, 6.30pm–9pm;
Sunday 12pm–2.15pm.

Red Lion PH
Peppard Common, Henley-on-Thames,
Oxfordshire
Tel: 01491 628329
Food-serving times: Monday–Saturday
12.30pm–3pm, 7pm–9pm;
Sunday 12.30pm–3.30pm.

St Nicholas's Church
Rotherfield Greys, Henley-on-Thames,
Oxfordshire
www.chord.demon.co.uk/greys/
Opening hours: daily 9.30am–4pm.

GREAT MISSENDEN, HUGHENDEN & HIGH WYCOMBE

Church of St Michael and All Angels
Valley Road, Hughenden Valley,
High Wycombe, Buckinghamshire
http://members.lycos.co.uk/Naphill/
hughenden-church.html
Opening hours: daily dawn–dusk.

Hughenden Manor
High Wycombe, Buckinghamshire
Tel: 01494 755573/65
www.nationaltrust.org.uk
Opening hours:
House, restaurant and tea-rooms March:
Saturday & Sunday 1pm–5pm;

April–October: Wednesday–Sunday
1pm–5pm.
Gardens March: Saturday & Sunday
12pm–5pm; April–October:
Wednesday–Sunday 12pm–5pm.
Park & Woodland daily.

Polecat Inn

170 Wycombe Road, Prestwood,
Great Missenden, Buckinghamshire
Tel: 01494 862253
Food-serving times: Monday–Saturday
12pm–2pm, 6.30pm–9pm;
Sunday 12pm–2pm.

White Lion PH

57 High Street, Great Missenden,
Buckinghamshire
Tel: 01494 862114
Food-serving times: Monday–Saturday
12pm–2pm; no food served Sunday.

BERKHAMSTED COMMON, ASHRIDGE HOUSE & FRITHSDEN BEECHES

Ashridge House

Ashridge, Berkhamsted, Hertfordshire
Tel: 01442 843491
www.ashridge.org.uk
Opening hours:
Grounds April–September: Saturday &
Sunday 2pm–6pm;
House not open to the public.

Berkhamsted Castle

Berkhamsted, Hertfordshire
Tel: 01442 871737 (keyholder)
www.english-heritage.org.uk
Opening Hours: Summer: daily
10am–6pm; Winter: daily 10am–4pm.

HARLINGTON, BUNYAN'S OAK & SHARPENHOE CLAPPERS

The Lynmore PH

Harlington Road, Sharpenhoe,

Bedford, Bedfordshire
Tel: 01582 881233
Food-serving times: Monday–Saturday
12pm–2pm, 6.30pm–9.30pm;
all day Sunday.

WATTON-AT-STONE, BENINGTON LORDSHIP & SACOMBE

All Saints' Church

Church Lane, Little Munden,
Hertfordshire
www.mundens.net/church/index.htm
Opening hours: by arrangement with
keyholder; details posted at church.

Bell Inn

4 Town Lane, Benington, Stevenage,
Hertfordshire
Tel: 01438 869270
www.bellbenington.co.uk
Food-serving times: Monday–Saturday
12pm–2pm, 7pm–9.30pm;
Sunday 12pm–2pm, 7pm–9pm.

Benington Lordship

Stevenage, Hertfordshire
Tel: 01438 869228/668
www.beningtonlordship.co.uk
Opening hours: all year by arrangement.

Boot Free House

Munden Road, Dane End, Ware,
Hertfordshire
Tel: 01920 438770
Food-serving times: Monday–Saturday
12pm–2pm, 6pm–8.30pm;
Sunday 1pm–3.30pm.

Church of St Andrew and St Mary

Church Lane, Watton-at-Stone,
Hertfordshire
Opening hours: Saturday morning, or
by arrangement with rectory (also
located on Church Lane).

George and Dragon PH
82 High Street, Watton-at-Stone,
Hertford, Hertfordshire
Tel: 01920 830285
Food-serving times: Monday–Saturday
12pm–2pm, 7pm–10pm;
Sunday 12pm–2pm.

St Catherine's Church
Nr Sacombe Green, Sacombe,
Hertfordshire
www.mundens.net/church/index.htm
Opening hours: by arrangement with
keyholder; details posted at church.

St Peter's Church
Church Green, Benington,
Stevenage, Hertfordshire
Opening hours: daily 9.30am–dusk.

BAYFORD, BRICKENDON, NEWGATE STREET & LITTLE BERKHAMSTED

Baker Arms PH
9 Ashendene Road, Bayford,
Hertford, Hertfordshire
Tel: 01992 511578
Food-serving times: Monday–Thursday
12pm–2pm, 6pm–9pm;
Friday 12pm–3pm, 6.30pm–9pm;
Saturday 12pm–3pm, 6pm–9pm;
Sunday 12pm–3pm.

Coach and Horses PH
61 Newgate Street Village,
Hertford, Hertfordshire
Tel: 01707 872326
Food-serving times: Monday–Saturday
12pm–3.30pm, 7pm–9pm;
Sunday 12pm–3.30pm.

Farmer's Boy PH
1 Brickendon Lane, Brickendon,
Hertford, Hertfordshire
Tel: 01992 511610
Food-serving times:
daily 12pm–9.30pm.

Five Horseshoes PH
1 Church Road, Little Berkhamsted,
Hertford, Hertfordshire
Tel: 01707 875055
Food serving times: Monday–Saturday
11am–10pm; Sunday 12pm–9.30pm.

NEWPORT, WIDDINGTON & DEBDEN

Fleur-de-Lys PH
High Street, Widdington,
Saffron Walden, Essex
Tel: 01799 540659
Food-serving times: daily
12pm–3.30pm, 7pm–9pm.

Mole Hall Wildlife Park
Widdington, Nr Saffron Walden, Essex
Tel: 01799 540400
www.molehall.co.uk
Opening hours:
Summer: daily 10.30am–6pm; Winter:
daily 10.30am–dusk.

Prior's Hall Barn
Widdington, Nr Newport, Essex
Tel: 01604 730320 (English Heritage)
www.english-heritage.org.uk
Opening hours: April–September:
Saturday & Sunday 10am–6pm.

White Horse Inn
Belmont Hill, Newport,
Saffron Walden, Essex
Tel: 01799 540002
No food served.

The White Hart
High Street, Debden, Essex

KELVEDON, COGGESHALL & FEERING

All Saints' Church
The Street, Feering, Colchester, Essex
Tel: 01376 570420/570437 (keyholders)
Opening hours: by arrangement with

keyholders.

Bell Inn
The Street, Feering, Colchester, Essex
Tel: 01376 570375
Food-serving times: Monday–Saturday
12pm–1.45pm, 6.30pm–9pm;
Sunday 12.30pm–2pm.

Church of St Peter-ad-Vincula
Church Street, Coggeshall,
Colchester, Essex

Coggeshall Grange Barn
Grange Hill, Coggeshall,
Colchester, Essex
Tel: 01376 562226
www.nationaltrust.org.uk
Opening hours: April–October:
Tuesday, Thursday & Sunday
2pm–5pm.

Paycocke's
West Street, Coggeshall,
Colchester, Essex
Tel: 01376 561305
www.nationaltrust.org.uk
Opening hours: April–October:
Tuesday, Thursday & Sunday
2pm–5.30pm.

Woolpack Inn
91 Church Street, Coggeshall,
Colchester, Essex
Tel: 01376 561235
Food-serving times: Tuesday–Friday
12pm–2pm, 6pm–9pm;
Saturday–Sunday 12.30pm–2pm;
no food served Monday.

INGATESTONE, BUTTSBURY & MOUNTNESSING HALL

Church of St Edmund and St Mary
Ingatestone High Street (nr Stock
Lane), Ingatestone, Essex
Tel: 01277 354550/353621 (church
wardens)

www.gregpotts.clara.net/stsmary-
edmundingatestone.html
Opening hours: Sunday during
services, or by arrangement with
church wardens.

Church of St Giles Mountnessing
Church Road, Mountnessing, Essex
Tel: 01277 352152 (keyholder)
www.stgilesmountnessing.co.uk
Opening hours: by arrangement with
keyholder.

Ingatestone Hall
Hall Lane, Ingatestone, Essex
Tel: 01277 353010
Opening hours: Easter–September:
Saturday, Sunday & Bank Holidays
1pm–6pm.

ROCHFORD & PAGLESHAM

Cherry Tree PH
Stambridge Road, Rochford, Essex
Tel: 01702 544426
Food-serving times: daily 12pm–2pm,
7pm–9.30pm.

Plough and Sail PH
Paglesham Eastend, Rochford, Essex
Tel: 01702 258242
Food-serving times: daily 12pm–2pm,
7pm–9pm.

Punch Bowl PH
Paglesham Churchend, Rochford, Essex
Tel: 01702 258376
Food-serving times: Monday–Saturday
12pm–2pm, 7pm–9pm;
Sunday 12pm–2pm, 7pm–8pm.

St Andrew's Church
Hall Road, Rochford, Essex

SHOREHAM, LULLINGSTONE & EYNSFORD

Eynsford Castle
Eynsford, Kent
Tel: 01322 863467 (English Heritage)
www.english-heritage.org.uk
Opening hours: March–September:
daily 10am–6pm;
October–February: daily 10am–4pm.

Lullingstone Castle
Eynsford, Dartford, Kent
Tel: 01322 862114
Opening hours: May–August:
Saturday & Sunday 2pm–6pm.

Lullingstone Roman Villa
Lullingstone Lane, Eynsford,
Dartford, Kent
Tel: 01322 863467 (English Heritage)
www.english-heritage.org.uk
Opening hours: April–September: daily
10am–6pm; October: daily 10am–5pm;
November–March: daily 10am–4pm.

Old Ford Tea Rooms
Riverside, Eynsford, Kent
Tel: 01322 861733
Opening hours: Monday–Friday
10am–4.30pm;
Saturday & Sunday 10am–5.30pm.

St Botolph's Church
Lullingstone, Sevenoaks, Kent
Opening hours: daily 9.30am–dusk.

Ye Olde George Inn
Church Street, Shoreham,
Sevenoaks, Kent
Tel: 01959 522017
Food-serving times: Tuesday–Saturday
12pm–3pm, 6pm–9pm;
Sunday 12pm–4pm;
no food served Monday.

TEYNHAM, CONYER & THE SWALE

Castle Free House
2 The Street, Oare, Faversham, Kent
Tel: 01795 533674
Food-serving times: Monday–Saturday
12pm–2.20pm; no food served Sunday.

St Mary's Church
Teynham, Kent
Tel: 01795 522510 (rectory)/521538
(church warden)
Opening hours: by arrangement with
rectory or church warden.

Ship Inn
12 Ospringe Street, Conyer,
Faversham, Kent
Tel: 01795 532408
Food-serving times: Monday–Thursday
12pm–2.30pm;
Friday–Sunday 12pm–7pm.

Three Mariners PH
2 Church Road, Oare, Faversham, Kent
Tel: 01795 533633
Food-serving times: Monday–Saturday
12pm–2pm; Sunday 12pm–3pm.

HOLLINGBOURNE, NORTH DOWNS WAY & THURNHAM

All Saints' Church
Upper Street, Hollingbourne,
Maidstone, Kent
Tel: 01622 880375/688830 (church
wardens)
Opening hours: daily 10am–4pm, or by
arrangement with church wardens.

Black Horse PH
Pilgrims' Way, Thurnham, Kent
Tel: 01622 737185
Food-serving times: Monday–Friday
12pm–2.15pm;
all day Saturday & Sunday.

Church of St Mary the Virgin
Thurnham, Maidstone, Kent
Opening hours: by arrangement with
church warden; details posted at
church.

Dirty Habit PH
Pilgrims' Way/Upper Street,
Hollingbourne, Maidstone, Kent
Tel: 01622 880880
Food-serving times: daily
11.45am–2.30pm, 6.30pm–9.30pm.

North Downs Way National Trail
Tel: 01622 221525 (North Downs Way
project manager)
www.national trails.gov.uk

CHARING, LITTLE CHART & PLUCKLEY

Black Horse PH
The Street, Pluckley, Ashford, Kent
Tel: 01233 840256
Food-serving times: Monday–Thursday
12pm–2.30pm, 6pm–10pm;
Friday & Saturday 12pm–9.30pm;
Sunday 12pm–4pm.

Church of St Peter and St Paul
Charing, Ashford, Kent
www.geocities.com/charingchristians/
Opening hours: daily 9.30am–dusk.

Royal Oak PH
The Street, Charing, Ashford, Kent
Tel: 01233 502218
Food-serving times: Monday–Saturday
12pm–2pm, 7pm–9pm;
Sunday 12pm–2.30pm.

St Nicholas's Church
Pluckley, Ashford, Kent
www.geocities.com/charingchristians/
Opening hours: daily, but best to visit
after 4pm (church also used as a
school classroom).

St Mary's Church
Little Chart, Ashford, Kent
www.geocities.com/charingchristians/
Opening hours: by arrangement with
keyholders; details posted at church.

Swan PH
The Street, Little Chart, Ashford, Kent
Tel: 01233 840702
Food-serving times: Monday–Saturday
12pm–2.30pm, 6.30pm–10pm;
Sunday 12pm–2.30pm, 7pm–9pm.

PADDOCK WOOD, HOP FARM COUNTRY PARK, RIVER MEDWAY & CAPEL

Church of St Thomas à Becket
Church Lane, Capel,
Nr Tonbridge, Kent
Tel: 020 7936 2285 (Churches
Conservation Trust)
www.visitchurches.org.uk
Opening hours: by arrangement with
Churches Conservation Trust.

Dovecote Inn
Alders Road, Capel, Nr Tonbridge, Kent
Tel: 01892 835966
Food-serving times: Monday–Saturday
12pm–2pm, 7pm–9pm;
Sunday 7pm–9pm.

Hop Farm Country Park
Beltring, Nr Paddock Wood, Kent
Tel: 01622 872068
www.thehopfarm.co.uk
Opening hours: daily 10am–5pm.

Hop Pocket Inn
59 Maidstone Road, Paddock Wood,
Tonbridge, Kent
Tel: 01892 832857
Food-serving times: all day
Monday–Saturday; Sunday 12pm–4pm.

Kings Head PH
Badsell Road, Five Oak Green,

Tonbridge, Kent
Tel: 01892 832070
Food-serving times: Monday–Saturday
12pm–2pm, 7pm–9pm; all day Sunday.

HEVER & CHIDDINGSTONE

Castle Inn
Chiddingstone, Edenbridge, Kent
Tel: 01892 870247
Food-serving times: Monday &
Wednesday–Saturday 12pm–2.30pm,
7pm–9.30pm; Sunday 12pm–2.30pm;
no food served Tuesday.

Chiddingstone Castle
Nr Edenbridge, Kent
Tel: 01892 870347
www.chiddingstone-castle.org.uk
Opening hours: June–September:
Wednesday–Friday 2pm–5.30pm,
Sunday 11.30am–5.30pm.

Hever Castle
The Estate Office, Hever,
Edenbridge, Kent
Tel: 01732 865224
www.hevercastle.co.uk
Opening hours:
Castle April–October: daily 12pm–6pm;
March & November: daily 12pm–4pm.
Gardens April–October: daily
11am–6pm; March & November: daily
11am–4pm.
Moat Restaurant March–November:
daily from 11am.
The Pavilion Restaurant daily from
11am.

King Henry VIII Inn
Hever Road, Hever, Edenbridge, Kent
Tel: 01732 862457
Food-serving times: Monday &
Wednesday–Saturday 12pm–1.45pm,
7pm–8.30pm; Sunday 12pm–1.45pm;
no food served Tuesday.

Rock Inn
Chiddingstone Heath,
Edenbridge, Kent
Tel: 01892 870296
Food-serving times: Monday–Saturday
12pm–2pm, 7pm–9pm;
Sunday 12pm–2pm.

St Mary's Church
Chiddingstone, Edenbridge, Kent
Tel: 01892 870478
Opening hours: daily 9am–dusk.

St Peter's Church
Hever, Edenbridge, Kent
Tel: 01342 850738/850277 (church
wardens)
Opening hours: daily 10am–5pm.

DORMANSLAND, HAXTED MILL & LINGFIELD

Church of St Peter and St Paul
Church Road, Lingfield,
Gatwick, Surrey
Tel: 01342 832519/832470 (church-
wardens)
www.lingfield.clara.net
Opening hours: daily 9am–4pm, or by
arrangement with churchwardens.

Haxted Watermill and Haxted Mill Riverside Brasserie
Haxted Road, Edenbridge, Kent
Tel: 01732 862914
www.haxtedmill.co.uk
Opening hours:
Watermill Easter–September:
Tuesday–Sunday 10am–2.45pm;
October–Easter: Sunday 10am–2.45pm.
Brasserie May–September:
Tuesday–Sunday lunch & dinner;
October–April: Wednesday–Sunday
lunch & dinner.

Plough Inn
44 Plough Road, Dormansland, Surrey
Tel: 01342 832933

Food-serving times: Monday–Friday
12pm–2.30pm, 6.30pm–9pm;
Saturday 12pm–2.30pm,
6.30pm–9.30pm; Sunday 12pm–6pm.

Star Inn
Church Road, Lingfield, Surrey
Tel: 01342 832364
www.starinnlingfield.co.uk
Food-serving times: Monday–Saturday
12pm–2.30pm, 6pm–9.30pm;
Sunday 12pm–3pm, 6pm–9.30pm.

BALCOMBE, ARDINGLY RESERVOIR & WAKEHURST PLACE

Ardingly Reservoir
The Lodge, Ardingly, West Sussex
Tel: 01444 892549
www.ardinglyactivitycentre.co.uk

Balcombe Tea Rooms
Bramble Hill, Balcombe, West Sussex
Tel: 01444 811777
Opening hours: Tuesday–Friday
10.30am–5pm;
Saturday & Sunday 11am–5pm.

Half Moon PH
Haywards Heath Road, Balcombe,
West Sussex
Tel: 01444 461227
Food-serving times: daily
12pm–2.30pm, 7pm–9.30pm.

St Peter's Church
Street Lane, Ardingly,
Haywards Heath, West Sussex
Opening hours: by arrangement with
rectory; details posted at church.

Wakehurst Place Royal Botanic Gardens and Mansion
Ardingly, Nr Haywards Heath,
West Sussex
Tel: 01444 894066
www.rbgkew.org.uk

Opening hours:
Gardens April–September: daily
10am–7pm; October: daily 10am–6pm;
November–January: daily 10am–4pm;
February: daily 10am–5pm;
March: daily 10am–6pm.
*Wakehurst Mansion, Wakehurst Place
Restaurant & Millennium Seed Bank*
April–September: daily 10am–6pm;
October: daily 10am–5pm;
November–January: daily 10am–3pm;
February: daily 10am–4pm;
March: daily 10am–5pm.

POLESDEN LACEY & RANMORE COMMON

Norbury Park Estate
Nr Dorking, Surrey
Tel: 08456 009009 (Surrey County Council)
www.surreycc.gov.uk
Opening hours: *Park* daily dawn–dusk.
House not open to the public.

Polesden Lacey
Great Bookham, Nr Dorking, Surrey
Tel: 01372 452048/458203
www.nationaltrust.org.uk
Opening hours:
House April–October:
Wednesday–Sunday 11am–5pm.
Gardens Summer: daily 11–6;
Winter: daily 11am–dusk.
Tea-room January–March & November:
Wednesday–Sunday 11am–4pm;
April–October: daily 11am–5pm;
December: daily 11am–4pm.
Festival last fortnight in June.

Ranmore Common
Nr Dorking, Surrey
Tel: 01372 453401 (National Trust)
www.nationaltrust.org.uk

Stepping Stones PH
Westhumble Street, Westhumble,
Nr Dorking, Surrey
Tel: 01306 889932

Food-serving times: Monday–Thursday & Saturday 12pm–2.30pm, 7pm–9pm; Friday 12pm–2.30pm, 7pm–9.30pm; Sunday 12pm–3pm.

Westhumble Chapel ruin
Westhumble, Nr Dorking, Surrey
Tel: 01372 453401 (National Trust)
www.nationaltrust.org.uk

SHERE, NORTH DOWNS WAY, ST MARTHA-ON-THE-HILL & PILGRIMS' WAY

Church of St Martha-on-the-Hill
Tillingbourne Valley, Guildford, Surrey
www.guildfordchurches.com/
Christchurch.htm
Opening hours: October–March:
Saturday 2pm–4pm,
Sunday 10.30am–4pm;
April–September: Wednesday
2pm–5pm, Saturday 2pm–5pm &
Sunday 10.30am–5pm.

New Barn Coffee Shop
Newlands Corner, Nr Albury,
Guildford, Surrey
Tel: 01483 222820
Opening hours: daily 8am–5.30pm.

Newlands Corner
Guildford Road, Nr Albury,
Guildford, Surrey
Tel: 01483 517595
Opening hours: daily, staffed on
Sunday.

North Downs Way National Trail
Tel: 01622 221525 (North Downs Way
project manager)
www.national trails.gov.uk

St James's Church
Shere, Guildford, Surrey
Opening hours: daily 8am–dusk.

White Horse PH
Middle Street, Shere, Guildford, Surrey
Tel: 01483 202518
Food-serving times: Monday–Saturday
11am–10pm; Sunday 12pm–10pm.

WANBOROUGH, COMPTON & THE HOG'S BACK

Good Intent PH
62 The Street, Puttenham,
Guildford, Surrey
Tel: 01483 810387
Food-serving times: Monday–Saturday
12pm–2pm, 7pm–9.30pm;
Sunday 12pm–2pm.

Harrow Inn
The Street, Compton, Guildford, Surrey
Tel: 01483 810379
Food-serving times: Monday–Saturday
2pm–3.30pm, 6pm–10pm;
Sunday 2pm–6pm.

Jolly Farmer restaurant
Puttenham Heath, Puttenham,
Guildford, Surrey
Tel: 01483 810374
Food-serving times: Monday–Friday
12pm–3pm, 5pm–9pm;
Saturday & Sunday 12pm–9pm.

St Bartholomew's Church
Wanborough, Guildford, Surrey
Opening hours: daily 9.30am–4.30pm.

St Nicholas's Church
Compton, Guildford, Surrey
Opening hours: by arrangement with
keyholder; details posted at church.

Wanborough Great Barn
Wanborough (off the Hog's Back),
Guildford, Surrey
Tel: 01483 444750 (Guildford Museum)
Opening hours: June–September:
first and third Saturday of each month
2pm–5pm.

Watts Gallery
Down Lane, Compton,
Guildford, Surrey
Tel: 01483 810235
www.wattsgallery.org.uk
Opening hours:
Gallery April–September: Monday,
Tuesday, Friday & Sunday 2pm–6pm,
Wednesday & Saturday 11am–1pm,
2pm–6pm, closed Thursday;
October–March: Monday, Tuesday,
Friday & Sunday 2pm–4pm,
Wednesday & Saturday 11am–1pm,
2pm–4pm, closed Thursday.
The Tea Shop daily 10.30am–5.30pm.

Withies PH
Withies Lane, Compton,
Guildford, Surrey
Tel: 01483 421158
Food-serving times: Monday–Saturday
12pm–2pm, 7pm–9.30pm;
Sunday 12pm–2pm.

LISS, SELBORNE & HANGERS WAY

Gilbert White's House and Garden and The Oates Museum
The Wakes, Selborne, Hampshire
Tel: 01420 511275
Opening hours: daily 11am–5pm.

Hawkley Inn
Pocock's Lane, Hawkley,
Liss, Hampshire
Tel: 01730 827205
Food-serving times: Monday–Saturday
12pm–2pm, 7pm–9.30pm;
Sunday 12pm–2pm.

The Queens Hotel
The Queens and The Limes Annexe,
Selborne, Hampshire
Tel: 01420 511454
www.queens-selbourne.co.uk
Food-serving times: daily until 9.30pm.

Selborne Arms
High Street, Selborne, Hampshire
Tel: 01420 511247
www.selbornearms.co.uk
Food-serving times: daily 12pm–2pm,
7pm–9pm.

OVERTON, HANNINGTON & WATERSHIP DOWN

Vine Inn
Hannington, Tadley, Hampshire
Tel: 01635 298525
Food-serving times: Monday–Friday
12pm–3pm, 6pm–9.30pm;
all day Saturday; Sunday
12pm–2.30pm.

STRATFIELD MORTIMER, SILCHESTER ROMAN TOWN & THE DEVIL'S HIGHWAY

Fox and Horn PH
The Street, Stratfield Mortimer,
Berkshire
Tel: 0118 933 2428
www.thefoxandhorn.co.uk
Food-serving times: Monday–Saturday
12pm–2pm, 6.30pm–10pm;
Sunday 12pm–3pm.

Old Elm Tree PH
Beech Hill Road, Beech Hill, Berkshire
Tel: 0118 988 3505
Food-serving times: Monday–Saturday
12pm–2.15pm, 7pm–9.15pm;
Sunday 12pm–9pm.

St Mary's Church
The Street, Stratfield Mortimer,
Berkshire
Tel: 0118 933 2001/3704 (church
wardens)
Opening hours: by arrangement with
church wardens.

INDEX

ACKNOWLEDGEMENTS

The author, **Christopher Somerville**, would like to thank his sister Louisa, who kindly checked several of the walks and saved him from quite a few mistakes.

New Holland Publishers would like to thank all members of staff and their friends who offered up their weekends to check the walks.

Picture Credits
All photographs by the author with the exception of the following:
Caroline Jones: front cover
Collections/Chris Cole: page 191
Collections/David M. Hughes: page 107
Collections/Paul Felix: page 187
Collections/Robert Pilgrim: page 179
John Bethell Photography: pages 21, 35, 51, 115
Pictures Colour Library Ltd: back cover, pages 123, 143, 151
Robert Hallman: pages 63, 85, 93, 167
Courtesy of South Bedfordshire District Council: page 43
Courtesy of Swale Borough Council: page 99
Swift Imagery: pages 29, 159
TravelInk/David Martyn Hughes: page 9
TravelInk/Ken Gibson: page 13